'Gripping and meticulously researched *Spectator*

'A compassionate account of her life' *Financial Times*

'Holmes's engaged and engaging book seeks to disentangle the real woman from this web of interpretations ... Her research is impeccable ... In telling Baartman's extraordinary story, Holmes's fascinating book illuminates the forces which dominated her age, and resound in our own' *Sunday Telegraph*

'Hers is a heartbreaking and important story' *Time Out*

'The most upsetting book I have read this year ... Holmes reconstructs this tragic life in its entirety ... with courage and sensitivity' *The Times*

'Holmes has done some excellent research not only into Saartjie's background but also into the London of the times ... Holmes has been meticulous in filling in the political background as well as the pseudo-scientific research leading to the so-called theory of eugenics' *Irish Times*

'Holmes's well-written account of Baartman's life and afterlife shows how an individual who led an extraordinary existence – and was a symbol of her century's tangled attitude towards sex, race and imperialism – lives on' *Sunday Times*

'A lively biography of Saartjie Baartman, a South African curiosity who achieved celebrity in early nineteenth-century London' *Daily Telegraph* Summer Reading Picks

'In this first post-colonial biography of Baartman, Holmes uses Saartje throughout, but musters as much factual information as possible, telling her tale with care and respect' *Independent*

RACHEL HOLMES is the author of *Sylvia Pankhurst: Natural Born Rebel*, *Eleanor Marx: A Life* and *The Secret Life of Dr James Barry*. She is co-editor of *Fifty Shades of Feminism* and *I Call Myself A Feminist*.

THE
HOTTENTOT
VENUS

THE HOTTENTOT VENUS

VENUS

The Life and Death of

SARAH BAARTMAN

RACHEL HOLMES

BLOOMSBURY PUBLISHING

LONDON · OXFORD · NEW YORK · NEW DELHI · SYDNEY

BLOOMSBURY PUBLISHING
Bloomsbury Publishing Plc
50 Bedford Square, London, WC1B 3DP, UK

BLOOMSBURY, BLOOMSBURY PUBLISHING and the Diana
logo are trademarks of Bloomsbury Publishing Plc

First published in Great Britain in 2007
This paperback edition published in 2020

Copyright © Rachel Holmes, 2007

A catalogue record for this book is available from the British Library

PB: 978-1-4088-9911-3; eBook: 978-1-4088-8151-4

2 4 6 8 10 9 7 5 3 1

Typeset by Palimpsest Book Production, Grangemouth, Stirlingshire
Printed and bound by CPI Group (UK) Ltd, Croydon, CR0 4YY

To find out more about our authors and books visit
www.bloomsbury.com and sign up for our newsletters

'And he said unto me, Son of man, can these bones live?
And I answered, O Lord God, thou knowest.'

Ezekiel 37.3

'The story of Sarah Baartman is the story of the African
people of our country in all their echelons.'

President Thabo Mbeki

'The rear end exists, I see no reason to be ashamed of it.
It's true that there are rear ends so stupid, so pretentious,
so insignificant, that they're only good for sitting on.'

Josephine Baker

'I am a sex-o-matic Venus freak when I'm with you.'

Macy Gray

CONTENTS

LIST OF ILLUSTRATIONS

Plates

'Love and Beauty', caricature engraving by Charles Williams from 1811, published in 1822. (*Bridgeman Images*)

A crowded street in London ('Grievances of London') by George Cruikshank. (*Getty Images*)

Coloured aquatint by Frederick Christian Lewis, published in March 1811, shortly before The Hottentot Venus went on tour. (*British Library Board. All Rights Reserved / Bridgeman Images*)

'Prospects of Prosperity', political cartoon by Charles Williams, 1810. (*British Museum*)

'The Three Graces', engraving by William Heath, 1810. (*British Museum*)

'Les Curieux en extase', unattributed cartoon, Paris, 1814. (*Royal Museums Greenwich Picture Library*)

Saartjie's state funeral, Hankey, Eastern Cape, 9 August 2002. (*Obed Zilwa / Trace Images*)

Images in the text

'Phoenomenon' poster from Daniel Lysons, *Collectanea; or a Collection of Advertisements and Paragraphs from Newspapers, Relating to Various Subjects*, vol. Iii, unpublished scrapbook. (*British Library Board. All Rights Reserved / Bridgeman Images*)

Barefoot Khoisan soldier. (© *Cape Town Archives Repository*)

Khoisan wet nurse and children, Cape Town, 1798, by Lady Anne Barnard. (*Courtesy of the National Library of South Africa: Cape Town campus*)

'House from which the female in Piccadilly Circus called The Hottentot Venus was taken – not 2 miles from Cape'. From a sketchbook of John Campbell, 1815. (*Reproduced by permission of Cape Town Archives Repository*)

'The Deformito-mania'. (*Chronicle / Alamy*)

'Neptune's Last Resource', cartoon by Charles Williams, 1811. (*British Museum*)

Saartjie's baptismal certificate, Manchester, December 1811. (© *MNHN, Paris*)

'Exhibition at Bullock's Museum of Bonaparte's Carriage taken at Waterloo', cartoon by Thomas Rowlandson, 1816. (*Alamy*)

'La Vénus Hottentote', cartoon by George Loftus, Paris, 1814. (*Royal Museums Greenwich Picture Library*)

Portrait by Nicolas Huet, 1815. (*Getty Images*)

Portrait by Jean-Baptiste Berré showing Saartjie covered, 1815. (*Getty Images*)

Coloured engraving and genital cartouche of Jean-Baptiste Berré's original 1815 portrait of Saartjie, showing her naked, published in 1819. (*Wellcome Library, London*)

A NOTE ON NAMING

Saartjie Baartman was born in South Africa in 1789. Her name is pronounced 'Saar-key', with a roll on the 'r'. Saartjie is an Afrikaans name and, like her surname, pure creole, the indigenous flowering of a name cross-fertilised by diverse languages and cultures. She may have been given a Khoisan name at birth, but it never entered written historical records. Throughout her short life she referred to herself as Saartjie.

Baartman, inherited from her father, means, literally, 'bearded man'. Saartjie translates into Little Sara, but the intensity of meanings created by the '-*tjie*' suffix is lost in English translation. This suffix makes a diminutive of a noun in Afrikaans. The construction derives from Dutch, in which the standard rule is to add '-*tje*' to a noun. Making a diminutive in Afrikaans has two different functions. It indicates smaller size, but it is also a powerful way of expressing sentiment. The key emotion expressed by the '-*tjie*' diminutive is endearment. Used between friends, family members, lovers and equals of all classes and races, it is a verbal demonstration of affection and care.

However, because using the diminutive form of a noun reduces the size of what it names, the '-tjie' suffix has also been used to subordinate and enforce servitude. Deployed in contexts where one individual assumed power over another – white to black, master to servant, male to female – this verbal miniaturising could express unequal power relations. During the colonial eras and apartheid, the '-tjie' suffix was often used by whites to indicate contempt, belittlement and domination over black people. In the politically infused and blood-soaked history of language oppression in South Africa, to mark a person's name with a diminutive therefore became, within this context, a racist speech act.

Saartjie Baartman is South Africa's most famous and revered national icon of the colonial era. As is usually the case with such iconic figures, there is some debate over her proper naming. Saartjie was known by several monikers during her lifetime, including the Christianised Sarah Bartmann.

Today the issue of her proper naming is divided between those who favour the Anglophone Sarah, or Sara, and those who think of her as Saartjie. To some, Sarah, or Sara, is a respectful honorific that distances her from the legacy of racism lingering in the diminutive applied to a tragic figure. For others, Saartjie is the fond evocation of her truest name, which emphasises her South African heritage. Although sometimes bitterly debated, both positions share the recognition that naming is one of the profound forms of power.

Saartjie was her name in life as she lived it.

NOW EXHIBITING

AT

N°· 225, Piccadilly,

NEAR

THE TOP OF THE HAY-MARKET,

From TWELVE 'till FOUR o'Clock.

Admittance, 2s. each.

THE

Hottentot Venus,

JUST ARRIVED FROM THE

INTERIOR OF AFRICA;

THE GREATEST

PHŒNOMENON

Ever exhibited in this Country;

Whose Stay in the Metropolis will be but short.

PHOENOMENON

Saartjie Baartman, stage-name 'The Hottentot Venus', emerged from behind a crimson velvet curtain, stepped out onto the three-foot-high stage in pointed green slippers adorned with black silk bows and surveyed her London audience with a bold stare. Her high cheekbones and dramatic greasepaint-and-soot make-up gave her a prophetic, enigmatic look. Smoke coiled upwards from the pipe firmly gripped in the side of her perfect Cupid's-bow mouth, drawing attention to her dimpled cheeks and heart-shaped face. It was a damp autumnal afternoon in London, the year was 1810, and Saartjie was a long, long way from home.

At 4 feet, 6$^{7}/_{12}$ inches in height,[1] she was a diminutive goddess. The springy pelt of her voluminous fur cloak draped from her shoulders to her feet, an African version of the corn-gold tresses of Botticelli's Venus – and every inch of its luxuriant, labial, curled hair was equally suggestive.

Light and dark faces peered back up at her. Saartjie saw their eyes dilate with wonder, then narrow again speculatively, as if uncertain how to evaluate the vision of this

African Venus arising before them out of the gleaming candlelight and fug of eye-watering smoke from the oil lamps illuminating the auditorium. Framing Saartjie, the audience could see a small grass hut and painted boards depicting pastoral African scenery and verdant, exotic plants. According to the posters that advertised the recent arrival of The Hottentot Venus in blazing colours and huge printed letters all over central London, these settings depicted the mysterious interior of Africa, although where exactly that might be, many in the crowd were not sure.

To the audience that gazed up curiously at Saartjie, Venus was simply a synonym for sex; to behold the figure of Venus, or to hear her name, was to be prompted to think about lust, or love. At the same time, the word *Hottentot* signified all that was strange, disturbing, alien and – possibly – sexually deviant. Some in the audience had heard or read travellers' tales of mysterious Hottentot women, reputed to have enormous buttocks and strangely elongated labia, and to smoke a great deal. And here she was, a fantasy made flesh, tinted gold by the stage light, elevated above them, uniting the full imaginary force of these two powerful myths: Hottentot and Venus. Her skin-tight, skin-coloured body stocking clung to her so snugly that it was plain for all to see that she wore no corset, stockings or drawers beneath. Most shockingly, the luminous ropes of ivory-coloured ostrich-eggshell beads that cascaded from her neck to her waist failed entirely to conceal her nipples, pert beneath the thin silken fabric.

The illuminated auditorium enabled Saartjie to see her audience almost as well as they could see her. She observed with great interest two men of distinctive appearance who entered the theatre together and gazed up at her in rapt fascination. One was statuesque, hawk-nosed and haughty looking. The other was stocky, with curly hair and twisted features. Though Saartjie did not know them, most of England did, and a murmur of recognition rippled through the crowd. The tall, grave-countenanced man was John Kemble, the nation's most famous actor, and the short man was the comedian Charles Mathews, celebrated as the best stand-up comic and impersonator in the land. Saartjie observed that Mathews had an odd facial tic; one of his eyebrows remained rigid while the other seesawed comically up and down. Kemble stared fixedly at Saartjie, in the manner described in the folk stories of her childhood as being like a lion looking at the moon. He was just on the point of approaching the stage to address her when suddenly a white woman elbowed forward, reached up and coolly pinched her, very hard. Shocked, Saartjie stooped down to push her assailant away, but as she did so, another fashionable female in a high-waisted Empire-line topcoat (so beloved of Jane Austen heroines) clambered up on to the stage and poked her sharply in the buttocks with her furled parasol, drawling that '. . . she wished to ascertain that all was . . . "nattral".'[2] Before Saartjie had the opportunity to defend herself, a smartly dressed gentleman joined forces with her ungentle, genteel aggressors and prodded her with his walking cane.

The Venus's manager, Hendrik Cesars, jumped up onto the stage and declared the show over for the afternoon. As the crowd dispersed, Kemble, muttering 'Poor, *poor* creature!',[3] stalked up to Cesars, protesting at the assaults on Saartjie, firing questions at him about her state of mind, comfort and well-being. The actor vehemently declined the manager's wheedling, pacifying encouragements to touch her, objecting, 'No, no, poor creature, no!'

Charles Mathews, who wrote up these events in his diary, observed that Saartjie watched the exchange between Kemble and Cesars attentively. 'She was,' he said, 'obviously very pleased; and, patting her hands together, and holding them up in evident admiration, uttered the unintelligible words, "O ma Babba! O ma Babba!",[4] gazing at the tragedian with unequivocal delight.' For a well-built woman, there was an unexpected daintiness and lightness to her gestures.

'What does she say, sir?' Kemble asked Cesars, 'Does she call me her *papa*?'

'No, sir,' the manager answered. 'She says you are a very fine man.'

Saartjie's dignified response to Kemble was a classic expression of *ubuntu*, the African philosophy of humanity, fellow-feeling, decorum and kindness. Her words signified respect and 'thanks' and clapping her hands was a courteous gesture of humility. Saartjie was offering appreciation to Kemble for his admiration and concern, and showing esteem for a man who, in her eyes, was a fatherly, and rather handsome, figure. 'Upon my word,' Kemble retorted, emphatically inhaling a pinch of snuff, 'the lady does me an infinite honour!'

The two entertainers left together: 'Now Mathews, my good fellow, do you know this is a sight which makes me *mel*ancholy. I dare say, now, they ill-use that poor creature! Good God – how very shocking!' Kemble and Mathews sauntered off down Piccadilly, in search of afternoon tea, speculating about Saartjie and her circumstances. However, just like the rest of the audience who had paid two shillings to gape at The Hottentot Venus that afternoon, they knew almost nothing about her.

Saartjie was twenty-one years old. Just six months previously, she had arrived in England on a ship from the Cape Colony, with a British military doctor named Alexander Dunlop, his South African manservant, Hendrik Cesars and a former black slave, whose name is not recorded, now apprenticed as Dunlop's servant. Saartjie lived with them in York Street, a short thoroughfare to the south of Piccadilly connecting Jermyn Street with St James's Square, and named in compliment to King James II. Saartjie's new home was at the heart of London's most fashionable district and a world away from her previous life.

A month prior to Mathews and Kemble's visit to Saartjie's show, on Wednesday, 12 September, Sir Joseph Banks, President of the Royal Society, had received an invitation[5] to attend an exclusive preview of The Hottentot Venus on the following Monday. This private view was to be held nearby, in 'the house of exhibition' at 225 Piccadilly, and the invitation was from Hendrik Cesars. Banks discovered that similar invitations had been sent to scientists, naturalists and fashionable members of high society, as well as diverse impresarios, including the now elderly playwright and politician Richard Brinsley Sheridan and William Bullock, famed manager of the Liverpool Museum, at the time London's best-selling attraction. On Thursday, 20 September, three days after the preview, an advertisement appeared in the *Morning Herald* and *Morning Post*, announcing the opening of London's latest curiosity to the public:

The Hottentot Venus. – Just arrived, and may be seen between the hours of one and five o'clock in the afternoon, at No 225, Piccadilly, from the banks of the river Gamtoos, on the borders of Kaffraria, in the interior of South Africa, a most correct and perfect specimen of that race of people. From this extraordinary phenomena of nature, the Public will have an opportunity of judging how far she exceeds any description given by historians of that tribe of the human race. She is habited in the dress of her country, with all the rude ornaments usually worn by those people. She has been seen by the principal Literati in this Metropolis, who were all greatly astonished, as well as highly gratified, with the sight of so wonderful a specimen of the human race. She has been brought to this country at a considerable expense by Hendrick Cesars, a native of the Cape, and their stay will be but short. To commence on Monday, the 24th instant. – Admittance 2s each.[6]

This hyperbolical advertisement, promising so much, in fact told very little. Yet it heralded the opening of London's most famous and controversial theatrical phenomenon of the winter of 1810. Almost overnight, The Hottentot Venus became the sensation of the metropolis, both on stage and off. Who was she, and where did she come from? And how did this young black woman who sang, danced and played the guitar come to be on the London stage, got up like a fetish and performing like a showgirl?

2

M TAI !NUERRE –
'MY MOTHER'S COUNTRY'[1]

Saartjie Baartman was born in 1789 in the Gamtoos River Valley, a lushly forested, semi-tropical estuary on the bitterly contested eastern frontier of the Cape Colony. Although Africa and Europe were worlds apart, the repercussions of that revolutionary year in Europe had a definitive impact on Saartjie's childhood.

She did not remember her mother, who died before Saartjie reached her first birthday. Amid the forgetful shadows of infancy this first loss was inchoate, but as an adult, her mother's death was an event to which Saartjie would always attach a precise date.[2] Last-born, she had four brothers and two sisters, who probably became responsible for her care. If she had substitute mothers – grandmother, stepmother or aunt – she never mentioned them. Saartjie's father, the dominant influence on her childhood, was a cattle drover and hunter, a late eighteenth-century South African frontier cowboy.

Beyond her immediate family, Saartjie's infant senses first

focused on an intensity of light, colour and sound. Hers was a childhood of jade mangrove, ochre earth, yellow veld, ultramarine skies, indigo ocean, blazing sun, relentless exposure to the elements, and hunger. Everywhere there was bright light, woodsmoke and birdsong. She heard the 'kok kok kok' of scarlet-winged louries, flocks of waders and pink flamingos, and the chatter of sugarbirds, stonechats, chorister robins and fork-tailed drongos, all mingled with the nervous rustle of bush-buck and garrulous vervet monkeys.

Today the scrubby Hankey-Patensie district, the forests and hills of Saartjie's homeland were then filled with the crash and roar of elephants and hunters' guns. Christian missionaries were a familiar presence. Lions were a constant threat. Saartjie, like all local children, grew up in a community alert to the constant danger of potentially fatal attacks by wild animals.[3]

There were really only two seasons. Summers were hot and humid, winters slightly milder. Rains dampened the firewood that Saartjie and her sisters carried home on their heads. Burning winds intensified the summer heat, blew cold in the winter, but never seemed to blow away the all-pervasive dust that got into everything: nostrils, ears, cooking pots of maize porridge and meat stew, and the straw thatch of the one-roomed shack in which the Baartman family lived.

The Gamtoos flows from the confluence of the Kouga and Groot rivers through green lagoons to the Indian Ocean. In Saartjie's day, tall bush still fringed the river-banks and coastline, and the tropical forests were filled with yellow-wood, sneezewood, thorn trees, wild fig and olive, impenetrably entangled with deep thickets of candelabra trees[4] and spekboom, favourite food of elephants. Lowland plains shelved towards the interior; deep valleys of thorn trees and open bushveld stretched between rocky escarpments and gorges. Visible for miles, the high hills were covered so densely with thickets of flame-red and orange aloes that when they flowered, the landscape looked ablaze.

Saartjie grew up within earshot of the rolling breakers of the ocean, but although palm-fringed and fertile, the land of her ancestors was no Edenic pastoral idyll: it was a war zone. Until the arrival of the European colonists at the Cape in the seventeenth century, the Gamtoos region was untroubled by Christian God or European law. However, by the time of Saartjie's infancy the eastern frontier had become a terrain of violent contest between indigenous and colonial groups. Her people, the Khoisan, were at the epicentre of this bitter struggle.

Saartjie was descended from the Eastern Cape Khoisan, the long-intermingled society of herding, pastoralist Khoekhoen (Khoi) and hunter-gathering, nomadic San, native to South Africa since prehistoric times.[5] Most scientists now agree that these groups were the world's first peoples, antecedents to us all.[6] For roughly two thousand years before Europeans set foot in southern Africa, Saartjie's ancestors occupied its western and southern regions. The Gamtoos was named by the Khoisan. Many regions, rivers, mountains, deserts, animals and plants in South Africa still bear Khoi names. For Saartjie, this was a familiar universe named for her by her father.

The genealogy of the Baartman family[7] passed through the long history of encounters between pre-colonial and colonial cultures at the Cape. In the seventeenth century, the Cape Khoisan clans were numerous, cattle-rich and autonomous, but by the last decades of the eighteenth century, their wealth had been all but annihilated. When the Europeans arrived, they had Bibles and the Khoisan had land; by the time of Saartjie's birth, the Khoisan had the Bibles, and the Europeans had most of the land. For more than 150 years the Western Cape Khoisan prevented invaders from European seafaring nations from establishing a foothold in South Africa. From the first Portuguese landing in 1488, the Khoekhoen held off the Portuguese, the Dutch, the English and the French. Finally, in 1652, the Dutch East India Company (VOC) established the first permanent settlement, a refreshment station in Table Bay, with Governor Jan van Riebeeck at the helm.

The Europeans forging a trading seaway to the east struggled, and failed, to master the Khoisan languages, particularly their complex phonology of implosive consonants, or 'clicks'. Khoisan dialects are unique in containing the largest inventory of consonants found in any known language. The intricate verbal arts of click-language-speaking peoples are regarded today as some of the most intriguing and beautiful in the world.[8]

Struggling with the clicks, the tongue-tied Europeans dubbed the Khoekhoen 'Hottentots', and the San 'Bushmen'. In the early days, these terms described different ways of life, not racial categories. The Europeans initially regarded the cattle-propertied Hottentots as trading partners, diplomatic and cultural go-betweens, and potential employees. The Bushmen, on the other hand, with their lack of livestock and ability to live from the 'bush', seemed elusive, inassimilable and insubordinate to a European value system of private property ownership and fixed settlement.[9] But in the end any distinctive cultural identity was construed as negative and inferior, and thus as a justification for conquest.

The legacy of these colonial categories was to cause confusion about Saartjie's identity both during her lifetime and afterwards. 'Hottentot' and 'Bushman' are among the most pejorative and contested terms in the lexicon of South African history. Jan van Riebeeck's opinion that Hottentots were 'a dull, stupid, lazy, stinking nation' who were 'bold thievish and not to be trusted' was long representative of the dominant European view of Khoisan people.[10] In the racial thinking of the nineteenth century, the economic and social differences between the Khoi and the San were transposed into differences of ethnic origin.[11] Over time, colonisers forced an association between 'Hottentots' and servility, 'Bushmen' and resistance. Invading Europeans fostered these divisions to make distinctions between 'good' (tractable) and 'bad' (resistant) natives in order to subordinate the Khoisan and repress their long history of armed struggle.

During the eighteenth century, the Eastern Cape Khoisan were squeezed into an ever-narrowing corridor of their ancestral lands by advancing settler-colonists. From the west came Europeans: traders, hunters, travellers, missionaries and, finally, cattle farmers. Also from the west came the Western Cape Khoisan, poor *trekboers* and colonial dissidents, driven away from the Dutch settlements due to intermarriage or illegitimacy, which banned them from land ownership in the colony. These latter groups were people of diverse ethnic origins whose ancestry bonded together slaves from Africa and Malaysia with white Europeans of all classes. From the east came the Xhosa, pushing westwards along the coast in search of new grazing and farming lands.[12] Many of the Eastern Cape Khoisan lived among the Xhosa, a legacy of the ancient trading routes that looped through the region. Long intermingled, the Khoisan-Xhosa of this region were known commonly by their unified names of the Gonacqua (or Gona) and the Gqunukwebe. By tradition the Xhosa had an open society, and advanced by assimilation and incorporation, so those who married or merged into the culture, and who spoke Xhosa, became Xhosa. The intermeshing between Khoisan and Xhosa culture is most evident in the deep relationship between their click languages. Poor *trekboers*, many of whom were already intermixed with indigenous Africans and imported slaves, had a similarly flexible attitude to integration. The Christian Dutch settler-farmers, however, with their Bibles and belief in private property, were an altogether different matter. Although they had no legal claim to the land they settled, and were nothing more than unregistered squatters, they resisted integration.

Among this diverse society of Khoekhoen, Xhosa, Sanqua, Gonacqua, *trekboers* and Christian Dutch were the imported slaves working for the settlers; some quite radical missionaries, including both European and African converts; and scholarly explorers and naturalists busy scribbling in their travel journals and sketchbooks. From infancy, Saartjie grew up amid Khoisan, Xhosa, Europeans and slaves settled down very close to one another. As one contemporary journal noted, from the outset '. . . kraals and European habitations were mixed.'[13] Most Xhosa farmers were more established, and wealthier in both cattle and culture, than the vagrant, shoeless Dutch *trekboers*.

A semi-autonomous community of Eastern Cape Khoisan, Saartjie's family among them, continued to live on their traditional grazing lands at the mouth of the Gamtoos. However, as their cattle stocks dwindled, they became increasingly dependent on wage labour, especially on the three surrounding farms, named after the rivers running through them: the Gamtoos, the Kabeljouws and the Loerie. In 1778 Saartjie's people were dispossessed when the government 'loaned' these farms to a Dutch farmer, Hilgert Muller. Muller and his henchmen went on a murderous land-grab; they ignored established grazing rights, stole cattle, occupied traditional Khoisan land, drove people from their homes, squatted villages, and raped and captured women and children, forcing them into concubinage and domestic service. The Gamtoos Khoisan were either compelled to work for the colonists or organised themselves into units of armed resistance, instigating cattle raids to regain their land and stock.

Saartjie grew up speaking Khoisan, and 'Low-' or 'Kitchen-Dutch' (Afrikaans) and, possibly, some Xhosa. She did not go to school, and never learned to read or write. Khoisan was an oral language, and Saartjie was already twelve years old when the first Khoisan spelling-book was printed by the London Missionary Society, of which she had no knowledge, and to which she had no access. Someone taught her to play music at an early age. She mastered the *ramkie*, a forerunner to the tin-can guitar, adapted specifically to blend Khoisan and Western folk-songs. She was adept on the single-string violin, or *mamokhorong*, important in Khoisan musical traditions involving dancing, and notoriously tricky to play.[14]

Because livestock ownership was central to Khoisan culture, they were expert herders and cattlemen. This made them desirable employees for Xhosa and Dutch farmers, for whom they worked as a means to try and rebuild their own depleted herds. The Khoisan had legendary abilities as horsemen and marksmen, and were highly prized war allies. Some Khoisan of the interior were skilled ivory-hunters, by which means they maintained some economic independence. The forests of the Gamtoos were rich elephant-hunting grounds. However, by the time of Saartjie's birth, many of the Gamtoos Khoisan had become indentured servants and workers on farms, earning their subsistence, cast-off clothing and, if lucky, a few head of cattle and sheep.[15]

Skilled cattlemen like Saartjie's father periodically served the Dutch East India Company working to provision the Cape Colony. In harvest and threshing season some of them hired themselves out to the farmers for a fixed fee.[16] Otherwise, they herded cattle, drove wagons or acted as hunting guides, and were paid in tobacco, cheap wine and sheep. The few head of livestock the Khoisan owned roamed long communal pastures, but grazing rights on land settled by white farmers became increasingly disputed.

On horseback, with a thick sheepskin covering his saddle, Saartjie's father must have looked imposing to his tiny daughter. He was a large figure in her world who comforted and provided for her but who was, from economic necessity, so often absent. She explained in later life that he was 'in the habit of going with Cattle from the interior to the Cape'.[17] This was a 900-mile round trip, and Baartman was away for long periods, returning with intriguing stories for his children about what he had seen at the faraway Cape. Between cattle runs, hunting expeditions and seasonal farm labour, he seemed to Saartjie to be always on the point of leaving, or just about to return.

Throughout Saartjie's childhood, the hills of the Gamtoos were filled with gunfire, smoke and fear. The so-called 'Bushman Wars' had escalated to an unprecedented level of ferocity. The Khoisan were pressurised on all sides. Boer commando raids deepened in horror and magnitude. The frontier ignited into widespread violence, with the Khoisan ranks joined by escaped slaves, white deserters and Khoi servants.[18] The rape and capture of children who would be forced to work as servants exacerbated the conflict.[19] Terrible atrocities often took place in these raids, including the violent murder of infants 'too young to be carried by the farmers for the purpose to use them as bondsmen'.[20] Entrapped Khoisan children were commonly sold in exchange for a horse, a gun or a pair of shoes.[21] Body parts such as the breasts of Khoisan women made into souvenir tobacco pouches were kept as trophies by Europeans.

When Saartjie was six years old, the British arrived, prompted by events in Napoleonic Europe. In the aftermath of the French Revolution, the free French republican armies helped the Dutch Republican Party to establish the Batavian Republic in Holland. Prince William and supporters of the House of Orange fled to monarchist-friendly England and persuaded the government there to take possession of the Cape Colony in order to prevent it from falling into republican French hands. In September 1795, following two months of fighting, the Dutch Governor surrendered the colony to the British.

Conveniently seizing the rhetoric of pro-French Jacobinism, the Dutch settlers rebelled against the occupation, and from 1795 to 1799 waged war on the British, determined to establish their own Boer republic in support of the Batavian regime. The British allied themselves with the military forces of the Xhosa and Khoisan, promising to restore their livestock and land, and to release them from servitude to the Dutch settlers. Many Gamtoos Khoisan cattlemen fought as mounted riflemen in the quashing of the Boer rebellion, and probably Saartjie's father was among them.

In 1799 the Khoisan and Xhosa militias defeated the Dutch, at which point their British allies promptly reneged on their

Barefoot Khoisan soldier.

promises, attempted to force the Xhosa back eastwards, and ignored Khoisan claims for land rights and autonomy. Furious at this betrayal, the Xhosa and Khoisan regrouped into fighting units which held fast in the hostile terrain they knew so well, determined to drive the British out of the eastern frontier. Khoisan hired hands and cowboys deserted from farms with their masters' horses and guns to join the fight[22] and win back their land. The British turned to their former Dutch enemies for assistance. For the colonists, this third frontier war of 1799–1802 was the most bloody and disastrous. The British and Dutch had armed the Xhosa and Khoisan themselves, by trading weapons for cattle. Through diverse alliances and successive wars, the Khoisan, Xhosa, runaway slaves and dissident whites of the eastern frontier sustained a long campaign of opposition to the colonial conquest of South Africa. Political and military pacts concluded between the Khoisan and the Xhosa in order to resist the colonists continued throughout the nineteenth century.

Stock theft in retaliation against settler encroachment was unrelenting. The Khoisan were seen as the most dangerous foes, feared equally by the Xhosa and the whites. Run ragged by stock theft and obligatory military service, many squatting white farmers were driven from the land. Simultaneously, pitted against each other by trade wars and desperation, the Khoisan raided their own neighbours.

These were the bewildering and terrifying events that shaped the landscape of Saartjie's upbringing. Amid the grand open vistas of the veld, the shady forests, long beaches and vaulted skies, children like Saartjie lived in the line of fire in a raw, frontier, intimately communal, hand-to-mouth existence.

In 1807, when she was seventeen or eighteen,[23] Saartjie's father was murdered. In 1810 she said her father was killed on one of his frequent cattle runs to the Cape. Baartman was, in Saartjie's words, 'killed by the "Bosjemen"' during a skirmish with what she described as a 'barbaric'[24] European-led commando unit. Intended to supply the Cape and enrich its colonial farmers, cattle runs were a prime target for many warring factions,[25] and it was almost impossible to distinguish between trading and commando raiding operations.[26] In 1815, however, an ailing, world-weary and champagne-drunk Saartjie recounted a more detailed story of her father's death to an equally inebriated Dutch-speaking French journalist. For all its embellishments and mawkish pathos, this account squares with the political realities of Saartjie's upbringing.

'My father,' she explained, 'was at the head of the hunters and my mother was the woman who organised the celebrations. Everyone sought to ally themselves with them, and I was greatly in demand.'[27] From among her many suitors, a young man named Solkar was the one who 'entered most deeply'[28] into her heart. Saartjie's parents organised a feast to celebrate their daughter's forthcoming marriage, and for a betrothal gift, Solkar gave Saartjie a tortoiseshell pendant.

The festivities lengthened into sunset:

> . . . the fires were lit on the hilltop. It was these very fires that betrayed us. We heard cries in the distance. We saw barbaric Europeans, and already in the midst of them were women struggling and refusing to follow in their footsteps.[29]

Saartjie and Solkar's betrothal party had fallen prey to a roving commando. Rifle shots blasted away the guitar, *goura* and reed-flute[30] melodies. Laughter turned to terrified screams. The men, led by the ardent young Solkar, threw themselves into battle against the commando raid.

The impassive sun returned in the morning, dispersing the cordite and sulphur-imbued mist. It revealed an abandoned hilltop, spilt human blood congealed with the fat of roasted meat, and the ash of trampled fires. Saartjie's father and her lover, Solkar, were dead. Overnight, her childhood was stolen. She had been captured, taken by the commando and forced, on foot, towards Cape Town.

At this point in her narrative, Saartjie kissed the tortoise-shell pendant round her neck and exclaimed,

> . . . all our defenders, our brothers, our lovers, all perished, and we unfortunate victims who did not die were tightly bound, and were taken away by the evildoers, far from our beloved forests, and driven, with a thousand insults, onto floating trees, where we saw nothing but the sea and the clouds.[31]

Saartjie wore the pendant for the rest of her life, and it is depicted in many of the images produced of her. This talisman is also recorded in the memory of a gesture, an etching in air. When subjected to the stress of public scrutiny by strangers, and at times of extreme vulnerability, Saartjie had an unconscious habit of repeatedly touching the pendant, 'which she often took in her two hands, pressing it hard against her lips and lifting her eyes to heaven'.[32]

Saartjie was orphaned, female and unprotected. In what can only be imagined as the most turbulent and distressing circumstances, she was wrenched from her home, separated from her remaining family, and taken into the custody of a hunter and trader named Pieter Willem Cesars, a free black (*vryswarte*) from Cape Town. How Pieter Cesars came into Saartjie's life, she never explained, nor has it yet been discovered.

The fact that Saartjie had reached puberty may have saved her life. Pieter Cesars's brother and sister-in-law were adopting a child and needed a wet-nurse, a service that was an unusual luxury for their class. Pieter Cesars decided to take Saartjie to the capital to become nursemaid to his soon-to-be adopted niece.[33] Whether Pieter Cesars was Saartjie's captor or her saviour remains one of the unsolved mysteries of her life. Hunters and traders were frequently involved in child-catching to sell children into service. Saartjie caught Pieter Cesars's attention; she was a good age for a nurse-maid, and a sharp and strikingly pretty youngster. By taking her into service with his family in the city, Pieter Cesars may have, albeit inadvertently, saved her from a worse fate, such as being murdered during the raid or indentured to one of the local white settler farms. For Saartjie, however, now a homeless teenager separated violently from all that was familiar, such distinctions might have seemed largely irrelevant.

The documentary evidence drawn from Saartjie's adult life reveals that her father's murder was the defining event of her youth.[34] Henceforward, the wishes of men dominated her life, because they held her in the grip of their economic and social power. Saartjie's relationship with paternalistic

Khoisan wet nurse and children, Cape Town, 1798, by Lady Anne Barnard.

figures was shadowed by her unresolved attachment to an idealised father, snatched from her at the point she most needed and respected him, and before she had cause to rebel against him.

Even at her tender age, Saartjie already had more knowledge than many better-educated children. She had witnessed the relentless resistance of her people to conquest. She encountered ruthless prejudice based upon bigoted notions about the inherent passivity, servility and inferiority of 'Hottentots'. However, Saartjie knew very well from personal experience that she was not the child of a passive people. Saartjie's upbringing was conditioned by opposition and conflict, but she had also witnessed concession and collaboration as responses to trade inducements, aggression and war. Her childhood was therefore an intimate education in the fine balance between the risks of resistance and the compromises of survival.

3

CITY OF LOST CHILDREN

Saartjie left the hills of flaming poker-red aloes with Pieter Cesars and trekked overland some 500 miles through the Breede River Valley and the Klein Karoo towards the great craggy ridge of the Hottentots Holland, the mountainous gateway between the south coast of Africa and the Cape Peninsula.[1] Pieter hunted and called at small settlements and trading posts along the way. To Saartjie, the month-long journey must have seemed interminable.

They skirted thickly wooded mountains filled with giant trees – yellow-wood, ironwood, stinkwood, alder, assegai – draped in knotty cloaks of monkey ropes,[2] their trunks rubbed smooth by elephants. By the end of the century, these deep, tree-filled kloofs would be decimated, turned into ships – or, as Saartjie put it, floating trees[3] – as well as railway sleepers, furniture and roof beams, to build an empire. At night, the bright four-star Southern Cross bisected the indigo sky. Saartjie, alone among strangers, was beyond the help of her dead parents or family. She watched: both out of curiosity and to survive.

Finally, they arrived at the Cape Peninsula, meeting point of two oceans. For Saartjie, Cape Town was a new, cosmopolitan world set in a sea of botanical green. So different from the war-torn ochre farmland and bitter, discarded scraps of settlement where she had grown up. The city was encircled by the giant's sweep of the Drakenstein Mountains, culminating in one of the world's most famous landmarks: the brooding, granite-purple Table Mountain and its buttressed escarpments forming the great, sweeping ampitheatre of the Table Valley. Filled with sails, Cape Town harbour was a jostling, bustling commotion of chandlery and the brisk traffic of fishing schooners, brigs, barks, fully rigged tall ships, warships and East Indiamen.

Saartjie had never before experienced humanity on such a scale. Somehow she needed to secure a foothold in this fast-flowing urban waterworld, a medley of diverse languages, peoples and crossed cultures. Cape Town's bustling hospitality prompted Captain James Cook to describe it in his journal as 'one great Inn fitted up for the reception of all comers and goers. Upon the whole there is perhaps not a place in the known World that can equal this in affording refreshments of all kinds to Shipping.'[4] Saartjie, however, had come to Cape Town not to be waited on but to serve. Pieter trusted that she could be tried out as a nursemaid. Besides, she had no choice; necessity should make her biddable. There was also about her something very appealing. Although extremely small, she had an air of compact-limbed strength and watchful composure.

Pieter Cesars lived in lodgings on Riebeek Street.[5] He had three young, motherless sons and one male Khoisan servant. He had no wife, but whether he was a bachelor or a widower is unclear. He kept no slaves.[6] Riebeek Street was situated just below the Company Gardens and nearby the Adderly Street Slave Lodge, in the business and administrative heart of Cape Town.

Saartjie was to live with Pieter's brother Hendrik and his family, just outside the city centre. Pieter took her to his brother's home, 'Not 2 miles from the Cape', in the Table Valley, later sketched by the missionary John Campbell as he passed by in 1815.[7] Campbell annotated his drawing as the 'House from which the Female in Piccadilly called the Hottentot Venus was taken' but failed to note its specific location. The sketch depicts a small, flat-roofed Malay-style white-washed stone cottage with the Moorish Mediterranean appearance typical of the region. Attached to the side were two *pondoks*,[8] low-walled lean-to extensions with a single sloping roof, providing rudimentary slave quarters for the Cesars' two domestic male slaves (*lyf-eigen-slaven*).[9] The cottage had

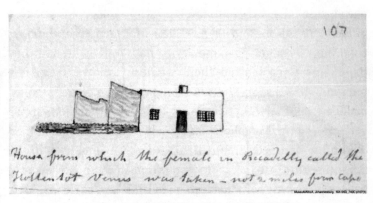

From a sketchbook of John Campbell, 1815.

a wooden door, internal shutters on the windows, and a chimney in the kitchen, which was the heart of the house.

And so Saartjie became live-in 'nursery maid'[10] to Hendrik and Anna Catharina's newly adopted daughter. The specific terms of her employment are not recorded. Before 1809, there was no legal wage structure for Khoisan domestic servants, and they were usually absorbed into households on an all-found shelter and food basis.[11] Female servants and slaves slept in the kitchen by the hearth, while male servants and slaves slept in outhouses. Saartjie might have slept on a mattress or skin on the packed-earth floor, which was sealed with cow-dung or oxblood.

In such a cottage, the kitchen was daily living-room, storeroom and overflow bedroom all in one. Soap and candles, tobacco rolls and slabs of dried fruit were stored in the rafters, from which hung maize cobs; salted, sundried strips of game or beef, and the thick, cured hide ropes used for making everything from harnesses to thongs for seats and beds. Released by the heat and mixed with the smoke from the fire, the thick smells of dried fruits, meats and cured hides filled the cottage.[12]

Hendrik Cesars and Anna Catharina Staal, 'both born in this remote corner',[13] had married in 1805.[14] The will they drew up shortly after their wedding shows that they expected to raise children.[15] However, there was a medical problem, and within two years the couple applied to the governors of the Orphan Chamber[16] to adopt a free child.[17] The Cape Town Orphan Chamber had been created in the seventeenth century to protect the needs and interests of free orphans. (There was no provision for slave orphans until 1815.[18]) From 1652 until 1819, the descent systems for both slavery and freedom at the Cape were matrilineal. This applied to everyone: slaves, free blacks and free citizens. The law of uterine descent meant that Anna Catharina could only pass her free-black status to her natural-born offspring or adopt a free child. Like Saartjie, little Anna Catharina had been an orphan, a common tragedy in Cape Town, which slavery had made a city of lost children.[19]

The 1807 Abolition of the Slave Trade Act abolished the slave trade in all British colonies and made it illegal to carry slaves in British ships, but existing slaves remained the property of their owners for life, and the latter could still dispense their futures as they saw fit. The Cape census of 1807,[20] ordered to make an official count of the number of slaves in the colony at the time of abolition, recorded that Hendrik and Anna owned two male life-slaves[21] but kept no female slaves. They also had three male Khoisan servants over sixteen and two female Khoisan servants over fourteen (described in the registers as 'Hottentot, *in dienst*': in service, or indentured). Saartjie was one of these 'indentured Hottentots'.

Colonial Cape Town had been a slave-owning society since the Dutch East India Company had made settlement in 1652.[22] In 1657 there were eleven slaves at the Cape: eight women and three men.[23] The following year, 170 Angolan slaves captured on a Portuguese ship were delivered to Table Bay. Slaves from Mozambique, Madagascar and Ceylon were imported thereafter, and by 1691 slaves numbered nearly 300, of which 44 were children. Most imported Cape slaves came from the Indian Ocean basin: the African east coast, Borneo and the shores of China. Among these were people of Abyssinian, Arabian, Bengali,

Borneose, Brazilian, Burmese, Chinese, Iranian, Japanese and Sinhalese origin.[24] At the close of the eighteenth century, mainland Africa and Madagascar had become the main sources of slaves, the majority of whom were landed at the Cape.[25]

During the first two decades of European settlement at the Cape, 75 per cent of all children born to slave mothers had white fathers, who could choose either to purchase their child's freedom or leave them in bondage.[26] Early Dutch colonial law forbade the enslavement of native South Africans, and custom prevented the enslavement of Europeans. In the early days of the Dutch colony, this meant that in cases where mixed-married parents were a native South African and a European, no legal distinction was made between their offspring and the children of Europeans. That the law was ignored is demonstrated by the gradual enslavement of the Khoisan over a period of two hundred years.

The Cape slave regime was based on Roman Dutch law, whereby the Roman categories of slavery were transposed into racial categories. Roman Dutch law was the legal system the Dutch colonists brought with them to the southern tip of Africa in 1652 from the province of Holland, whose laws and procedures derived directly from the sixth-century Justinian codification of ancient Roman law, as ardently developed by mediaeval scholars and commentators. Because it antedated the Napoleonic conquest of the Netherlands, it was uncodified, and was soon subjected to extensive practical procedural implants from the British, who took over the administration of the Cape in 1806. Since all slaves were ipso facto black, freed slaves were designated free blacks at the Cape even if descended from a European parent.[27] Blackness therefore was not so much a matter of skin colour as of non-European descent.[28]

The free blacks were the most urbanised and poorest of all the slave owners, making their family structure and slave-owning behaviour substantially different from that of other, richer groups.[29] Hendrik Cesars was an illiterate manservant,[30] employed by a British Army medical officer named Alexander Dunlop, Staff Surgeon to the 38th South Staffordshire Regiment of Foot and Chief Surgeon of the Slave Lodge. Anna Catharina was literate, and for all that the Cesars had sufficient means to adopt a child, keep slaves and Khoisan servants, and draw up legal documents, they lived communally in a humble cottage where collective shrift was necessary to sustain the household and its dependents.

Cesars, or Cezars, from Caesar, is a name rooted in Romance rather than Germanic languages. South African genealogies list no Cesars, in any variation of spelling, among any of the old European South African settler families.[31] However, Caesar, Cesar and Cezars were very common slave names at the Cape from the 1700s.[32] Anna Catharina was probably related to the Staals of Amsterdam who immigrated to the Cape in the eighteenth century.[33]

The 1807 census registered Hendrick and Anna Catherina as free blacks. Legally, the term 'free black' covered three main subgroups of the burghers. All liberated slaves (described as manumitted) entered the free-black community, but not all free blacks were descended from slaves. A significant proportion came from the population of convicts (mostly Indo-Chinese, Indonesian or Sinhalese) and political exiles (predominantly Indonesian, many royal or high-born) transported to the Cape.[34] Among the prisoners of war brought there were priests and princes of Muslim states subverted or overthrown by the Dutch East India Company. The remaining population of this group comprised ex-slaves and locally born free blacks third-, second- or first-generation descended from 'interracial' unions.

Estimates based on the British census[35] suggest that in 1807 there were about 1,200 free blacks in the Cape Colony as a whole, so the Cesars brothers were part of a small but significant population. From the eighteenth century, Islam and Christianity dominated monotheistic religious belief. Muslim observance expanded significantly among the ex-slave population, partly due to the willingness of Muslim clerics to marry and recognise the unions of ex-slaves, whereas the Christian churches, both Catholic and Protestant, refused its priests this toleration.

Free blacks preferred to live in Cape Town in the eighteenth century because there were more opportunities for making a living than in the hinterland. Poor whites had pressurised freed blacks out of most occupations as early as the 1720s. They worked in the port, especially on barges and lighter sea traffic, and in fishing, candle making and small retailing.[36] Free blacks and freed slaves could legally own property but were in reality often too impoverished to buy land or houses, a problem compounded by the refusal of lenders and banks to extend them credit. This in turn generally excluded them from agriculture. They tended to become modest wage labourers or traders who rented their homes or smallholdings.

Transfer records show that slaves and free blacks frequently utilised the slave market to liberate themselves and their enslaved relatives, lovers and community members. From 1658 to emancipation, from a disadvantaged, humble economic base, free blacks manumitted 18 per cent of all those released from slavery, the most slaves per capita of any group of slave owners.[37] Hard toil and scraped-together savings were used to free relatives, friends and community members, sacrifices which pushed many into interminable poverty.

Saartjie's overcrowded mixed household was a microcosm of the diversity of Cape Town. Even if she had been a minor, rather than a teenager, there would have been no government record of her transfer to the Cesarses' employ, because there was no formal process for registering orphaned Khoisan or slave children. In the eyes of the law they did not exist.[38]

The legal technicalities that distinguished enserfed dependent from human chattel had a direct impact on Saartjie. Economically, sexually and racially, she was unfree. However, her arrival in Cape Town coincided with the transition of the colony from Dutch Republican to British rule, and with the changes in the slave trade that accompanied that shift. The question of Saartjie's freedom was to make her a living example in an international argument about the rights of man and woman that was reshaping the early nineteenth-century world.

While Saartjie adjusted to urban life, missionaries and pro-abolitionist sympathisers were starting to challenge a 300-year-old mythical stereotype about the savagery and barbarism of South Africa's indigenous peoples. This

challenge had its origins in the eighteenth century, in the
philosophical objections of thinkers such as Rousseau to the
depiction of the Khoisan as sub-humans, the missing link
between civilised man and bestial apes.[39] Diderot, whose
Encylopedia described 'Hottentots' in racist and abject terms
as 'the most barbarous savages'[40] made a rhetorical appeal
to Khoisan people about the dangers of advancing white
men: 'Flee, unfortunate Hottentots, flee! Hide yourselves in
the forest . . . The tiger will eat you perhaps; but he will
take only your life. The other will ravage your innocence
and your liberty.'[41] Diderot's sentimental and patronising
account ignored the fact that colonisation had already
ravaged the Khoisan long before Saartjie was born.

John Campbell, the missionary who sketched Saartjie's
home, recorded being waited on by Hottentot servants at
a lavish dinner at Genadendal. He commented that '. . .
[t]hey did every thing with as much propriety and expedition as our best English servants could have done.'[42]
Campbell's experience of the grandeur of a Dutch family in
their gabled house was a long way from Saartjie's life as a
maidservant to the Cesars in their overcrowded cottage.
Numerous sensationalised travel accounts written by
European explorers rejected the Khoisan as abject and
uncivilised, distorting the realities of life in the urbanised
mixed communities of Cape Town. Campbell challenged
these anachronisms, arguing that the Khoisan were amiable
peasants and far cleaner and less violent than proletarian
Londoners:

> The Hottentots, who are the aborigines of this country, are a
> people nearly extinct; a few kraals only remaining within the

limits of the colony. They are far from being so barbarous a race as they are usually supposed to be by Europeans, who in their ordinary talk will say, 'As wild as a Hottentot' – 'as savage as a Hottentot, &c.' just as they say, 'As rich as a Jew' – 'as cunning as a Jew'. They have nothing more savage about them than the peasantry in England. I have seen families in London living in hovels more dirty than ever I saw occupied by Hottentots, and many in London have committed more atrocious deeds than any I have ever heard the Hottentots charged with. I think the Hottentot mind is better cultivated than the minds of many in the lowest ranks in London; and I should expect to be much better served, and to be more safe in travelling with twenty Hottentots, than with twenty Europeans.[43]

Saartjie's duties revolved around taking care of little Anna Catharina as well as domestic labour, washing, cleaning and assisting with the cooking. It was common practice for Cape settler women to use female slaves as wet nurses for their infants, in order to increase their own fertility,[44] but it was unusual for poorer families to employ a nursemaid to suckle their infants. Saartjie, however, could not have wet-nursed were it not that she had a baby of her own. Due to the free-black status of her employers, her world was more permeable than it would have been had she worked for a higher-class, white settler family. Initially, her social life was an extension of her domestic responsibilities: snatched moments of liberty when running errands, and looking after little Anna Catherina and Pieter Cesars's sons on Sundays, when the entire household attended church.

Hendrik and Anna Catharina were practising Christians.[45] Sunday services provided Saartjie with one of her first opportunities to make friends and acquaintances of her own. The Gamtoos River Valley of her childhood had rustled with the turning pages of missionary Bibles. Noted Christian converts existed among the Khoisan at the turn of the century, among them lay leaders like Cupido Kakkelak, 'Samson', Hendrik Boesak and Jochem Vogel who preached on the farms where they could get permission, and to those living in the bush along the Sundays, Gamtoos and Bushman rivers.[46] But Saartjie was not baptised until after she left the Cape.

Besides church, other intriguing opportunities for a teenager recently arrived from the provinces were provided by the communion of working people in altogether different places for venerating wine and flesh: the taverns, inns, alehouses and shebeens clustered around the harbour and tucked into every street of the expanding city. Hendrik's master, Alexander Dunlop, regarded by his fellow officers as a talented but renegade miscreant,[47] was an exuberant frequenter of the tippling houses, and was known for his love of carousing with his social inferiors, particularly his manservant Hendrik.

Tavern nightlife was Saartjie's first small space of freedom. Her ability to play, sing and dance made her popular. Sailors and the poorer servants of empire filled these tap-houses, bringing with them sea shanties and folk-songs which were blended with Khoisan and slave musical traditions. During her first year in Cape Town, Saartjie fell for a young soldier whom she met, possibly, in church or at a tavern. His name is lost, but the resonant echo of a drumbeat locates Saartjie's lover as a regimental drummer attached to the Cape Town garrison.[48] Their shared love of music was doubtless a mutual attraction – that, and Saartjie's predilection for masculine figures with an arresting presence. British Army drummers traditionally had showy, distinctive dress and battle uniforms, typically white trousers and a scarlet tunic topped by a gaily bedecked turban. The duties of a drummer in an infantry regiment required some rhythmic talent and either a fairly imposing physique or a great deal of energetic enthusiasm.

Saartjie's drummer had musicality and boyish charm wrapped in the alluring package of a uniformed soldier. Drummers were the beat-keepers of the march, and battle signals were mostly performed on the drum. In garrison, drummers were the company's, regiment's, brigade's or Army's clock: commands on the drum included the call to camp duty, the church call and the call to the parade-ground. Drummers were also the regimental alarm clock, responsible for the sunrise reveille, a task that made them unpopular with other soldiers.

In addition to their military duties, regimental musicians officiated at formal civil functions and featured among Cape Town's popular entertainers. Military musicians were much in demand in church, at weddings, at parties and as part of tavern nightlife. In the egalitarian atmosphere of multiracial shebeens, the poorer classes of many continents rubbed shoulders, playing together and adapting their instruments. Sharing diverse musical traditions from Africa, Europe, the east, they forged the foundations of the musical fusion that has become Cape Town's unique sound.

The encounter between Saartjie and her drummer boy quickly developed beyond high-spirited nights in the smoke-filled shebeens. The couple soon contrived to live together

despite their modest means. Saartjie moved in with her new
lover. The British regiments were garrisoned at Cape Town
Castle and in a large barracks located a block north of the
Parade. By tradition, prostitutes, girlfriends and wives
shared quarters with their men. Lowly drummers were
billeted in dormitory barracks, where rough blanket dividers
provided the only privacy.

Saartjie continued to work for Hendrik and Anna
Catharina.[49] As she was no longer living with them, she
lost the benefits of being a live-in servant. However, the
drummer's monthly wage sufficed for them both, although
war-related inflation made the city expensive.[50] His duty to
wake the regiment ensured that Saartjie could rise early and
get to work on time.

Little is known about Saartjie's drummer. According to
the London *Morning Herald*, he was Irish.[51] Napoleon's
surgeon Georges Cuvier who later met her in Paris claimed
that Saartjie 'said that she had been married to a Negro'.[52]
It is possible that her lover may have been a local Khoisan
boy in the Cape Regiment or an Nguni volunteer.[53] There
had been indigenous regiments attached to the Dutch, and
then British, services since the eighteenth century. The
'Hottentot' regiments – or Pandours, as they had previously
been known, included mounted riflemen and light infantry
– in 1806, after they had assisted the British to regain the
Cape, these regiments were disbanded and absorbed into
the regular British service. It is equally possible that
Saartjie's drummer was West Indian or a former slave
posted to the drums in exchange for the promise of freedom.
Since the fourteenth century, there had been black musicians and percussionists in the British Army. In the

eighteenth century it was the fashion among many regiments to employ drummers from Africa and the West Indies. Black Guardsmen were familiar figures to early nineteenth-century Londoners, having been part of the daily ceremony of the Changing of the Guard since the time of the Court of St James.

The 93rd Sutherland Highlanders of Foot garrisoned at the Cape Castle from 1806 to 1814 had played a key role in the recapture of the Cape Colony from the Dutch. The 93rd embarked on the expedition to Table Bay from the cove of Cork in July 1805, thus providing one explanation for the claim that Saartjie's drummer might have been Irish. The Highland regiments also had a long, venerable tradition of enlisting African musicians. Furthermore, Alexander Dunlop's regiment, part of the British forces that captured the Cape, obtained most of its drummers from the West Indies, due to its having been stationed there for almost sixty years until 1765. Whether Irish, West Indian, Khoisan, Nguni or a slave made free through military service, the certain fact is that Saartjie's lover was a regimental drummer in the British Army.

In Cape Town, Saartjie, on the arm of her soldier, first encountered the flavours of Napoleonic Europe. Watched with admiration by his new girlfriend, the drummer played in military parades attended by the privileged echelons of a European society very different from the foot soldiers of empire Saartjie encountered in the taverns. Walking out together, she and her lover watched from the sidelines as the vanity fair of moneyed society paraded the streets and promenaded in the manicured Company Gardens at the city's heart.

European visitors often remarked on the manners and fashions of Georgian Cape Town, contrasting its urbane hospitality with the unnerving wilderness beyond. Some years earlier, in 1796, a young soldier stationed at the Cape, William Jones, had written a letter to his uncle in Dorsetshire, the Reverend Bowyer Edward Sparke. (By coincidence, fifteen years later Reverend Sparke would play a decisive role in Saartjie's life.) Jones's letter described the usual picaresque adventures of a journey to the South African interior, 'an enchanted place' with 'stupendous' mountains, 'beautiful shrubs', 'excellent' farmhouses, 'indolent' Hottentots 'sleeping almost the whole day'[54] and so on. Sniffy about the 'wretched' and 'filthy' manner in which the Khoisan lived, Jones was nevertheless intrigued by the women,

> . . . ornamented with small beads, shells and other trinkets they pick up; whose chief amusement appears to be playing on a sort of guitar, which has 3 strings, the body of it is made from a scoop'd Pumpkin, they hold it when playing close to their chin; and keep time unless dancing, by a motion of the body backwards and forwards; I have heard them play several times, but always the same tune, which is plaintive, & pretty.[55]

Jones was surprised to discover that 'they all of them now speak Dutch; their native language is I believe almost totally forgotten.' Back in Cape Town, he turned his attention to the exotic plumage of the Dutch and English women:

> Do you know it is now a difficult matter to distinguish a Dutch Lady, from an English? Short Waists, and the Hair quite a la

mode Anglois; the men are still *idiots* and dress as unbecoming as ever. The Company's Gardens are quite the Kensington of the place, the Ladies and Gentlemen walk there every evening after the sun is down; and it only wants lamps to make you imagine yourself near London. If Ostrich feathers can make Ladies fine, here they are in perfection.[56]

Saartjie and her lover observed these rich whites enjoying themselves, perhaps little imagining it could be possible that in just a few years, Saartjie would herself live in a lamplit street in London's most fashionable quarter and ride in a carriage around Kensington Gardens in her own gowns and ostrich feathers, peeping out at the leisurely strolling classes who strained to get a glimpse of her.

The pleasures shared between Saartjie and her drummer soon led to their conventional outcome when, in 1807, she realised that she was pregnant. The pregnancy was successful, and, less conventionally, her young soldier took responsibility for the child. For two years, Saartjie had a new family. It was during this period that she wet-nursed little Anna Catharina Cesars, following the common practice of Khoisan and slave nursemaids breastfeeding first their own children and then their employers, without a break, so that their milk did not dry up. Hendrik and Anna's need for a wet nurse gave them reason to encourage Saartjie's relationship with the drummer, and to support the birth of her child.

Then tragedy struck again. Just before his or her second birthday, Saartjie's infant became desperately ill. Khoisan patients were treated at the Slave Lodge, where Alexander Dunlop was Chief Surgeon; it is likely that Hendrik asked his master to treat Saartjie's first-born. But to no avail. 'The child is since dead'[57] was Saartjie's choked, stark epitaph to this irreparable loss. Yet again, family had been snatched from her. There is no record of the baby's name, or of why she or he died; the commonest causes of Khoisan infant mortality in Cape Town during this period are not documented.

How different Saartjie's life might have been had her child lived. Her relationship did not withstand this calamity. She and her drummer were young and had not known one another very long. It is unclear whether the drummer left Saartjie, possibly sent to another posting, or she him. For the short term, they had a fun, and seemingly loving, interlude. Maybe an itinerant drummer boy had little that a girl could count on for the long term. Or perhaps they could not adequately console each other for their baby's death. Saartjie had lost her mother as an infant; now her own child was dead. Following their bereavement, the drummer disappeared from Saartjie's life, and from the historical record. With this triple blow, Saartjie lost her firstborn, her lover and the family she had sought to rebuild. Saartjie was once again in a precarious position. Her livelihood depended upon her ability to wet-nurse Anna Catharina, and on her drummer's wages. Aged twenty-one, Saartjie was uncertain of her future value to the Cesars, and her survival hung in the balance.

4

STOWAWAY

By the end of 1809, Saartjie's life had narrowed once again to domestic drudgery. The Cesars kept her on as nursemaid and servant, and she moved back into their cottage. While grieving for her own child, Saartjie had to continue to look after little Anna Catharina. Only she knew the depths and demands of the pain that must have caused. It seemed increasingly that her value lay in her body and in the services it could provide to others.

Two unrelated events in 1809 catalysed Saartjie's future. The first was the issuing of the new 'Hottentot Proclamation' by the colonial government. The second was that Alexander Dunlop, on whom the Cesars' household depended, lost his job.

The Hottentot Proclamation was issued by the Earl of Caledon, third British Governor of the Cape. This notorious piece of colonial legislation for the first time permitted the Khoisan to be legally indentured.[1] The measure attempted, and failed, to address two irreconcilable problems. The colony had a labour shortage, exacerbated by the abolition

of the slave trade in 1808. White Boers in particular, still
bitter about the Khoisan rebellion of 1799–1803, complained
about the labour scarcity. Simultaneously, missionaries
protested about the Khoisan's social and economic conditions, and argued for improvements in their judicial status.[2]
Inevitably, the effects of the Hottentot Proclamation proved
contradictory. Ostensibly, it tried to improve the legal status
of the Khoisan by including them under the rule of law, but
in doing so, it introduced draconian constraints on their
movements and gave white masters unprecedented legal
control over their Khoisan servants.

Hendrik and Anna Catharina were now required to officially register all the Khoisan members of their household.
In compliance with the proclamation, Saartjie was taken
before a magistrate and formally indentured as a 'Hottentot'
servant. Technically, this formal registration entitled her to
a wage and some basic conditions of employment. In reality,
the colonial government put little effort into monitoring
the now 'protected' interests of the Khoisan. In the
Proclamation's revealing words, the Prospero-like Lord
Caledon 'extend [ed] his peculiar protection in nature of a
guardian over the Hottentot nation under his government,
by reason of their general imbecile state'.[3] Saartjie was now
more vulnerable to exploitation, as well as being subject to
the authority of an absolute paternalism allegedly designed
to protect her welfare.

During the same year that Saartjie's child died, Dunlop
had been pitched headlong into a professional crisis. He
lived in bachelor's lodgings in the heart of Cape Town at
28 Wale Street,[4] next door to the Slave Lodge, St George's
Cathedral and the Company Gardens. Dunlop had joined

the 38th Regiment of Foot as Surgeon's Mate in January 1792, had been gazetted Surgeon in August 1796, and had become a Staff Surgeon in August 1803.[5] In 1806, when the British captured the Cape, he was appointed military Staff Surgeon at the Army General Hospital in Cape Town and simultaneously given the civil office of Chief Surgeon of the Slave Lodge,[6] which since 1685 had provided medical treatment for slaves, Khoisan, prostitutes and other groups excluded from care in the civil and military hospitals. The Slave Lodge was overcrowded, in urgent need of repair and woefully under-resourced.[7]

Dunlop had a reputation for considerable skill as a physician. He was undiplomatic to his superiors and well known in Cape Town for courting controversy. Laurence Hynes Halloran, Chaplain to Her Majesty's Forces at the Cape, held Dunlop responsible for betraying a pair of duellists on Christmas Day 1809. The weather was oppressively hot, wine flowed freely, tempers boiled over. Paymaster Patello received 'a slight flesh wound', which Dunlop dressed. The duellists begged him to keep their vow of secrecy (the duel was illegal), but, Reverend Halloran expostulated, Dunlop 'gave such Publicity to the Circumstances of the Duel that it became known to Lieutenant General Grey, who immediately ordr'd a Court Martial!'[8]

In 1809 Dunlop became embroiled in a dispute with the colonial authorities over the treatment of sick Khoisan women at the Slave Lodge. From the beginning of the British occupation, all sick Khoisan were referred to the Slave Lodge hospital, but there was no provision for treating women with venereal illnesses. In 1808 there was an alarming increase in the spread of sexually transmitted diseases among the troops, convicts, prisoners and prison guards. Prostitutes were, of course, blamed, and Khoisan women were singled out for particular censure. Dunlop and Dr Hussey (Inspector of Hospitals and chief of the General Hospital) highlighted the need to treat 'diseased Hottentot Women'[9] and urged the government to take measures to separate them from the troops: '. . . for your information . . . the health of the Troops in Camp is suffering materially from their intercourse with loose and disorderly Women (principally Hottentots) who frequent the neighbourhood of [the] Camp.'[10]

However, the administration procrastinated and in return for this inaction got a venereal epidemic. Finally, on 1 April 1809, a part of the slave hospital was appropriated 'for the accommodation of sick Hottentots and others', and the women were separated from the regular troops, under Dunlop's responsibility. The administration committed itself to covering the additional costs for their treatment at the Slave Lodge, but two months later Dunlop had yet to receive the new grant. He raised the matter with the Governor's office, requesting 'such allowance as you may think proper for the medical care of those people'[11] and pointing out that he could not pay the costs out of the small military stipend he received for his medical superintendence of the Slave Lodge. In January 1810, he submitted a total claim for 305 rix dollars – a very large sum of money.[12]

However, regarding itself as merely temporary custodian of the Cape on behalf of the exiled Prince of Orange, the parsimonious British government was unwilling to expend a penny more than necessary on housekeeping in the colony, and refused to pay. Moreover, it ruled 'any charge whatever with regard to Venereal Female Hottentots as altogether inadmissible'.[13] Dunlop, they stated, had willfully misunderstood his instructions.

Dunlop's vociferous protests provoked General Grey to complain about his conduct directly to the Governor, whom he begged not to 'pay one sixpence of the bill'. Dunlop received a strong reprimand, and General Grey threatened that 'if he gives further trouble I shall name another medical officer to his situation'.[14] Give further trouble is exactly what Dunlop did. Within the month he was placed on transfer back to England, and General Grey was looking for a replacement for both of his posts.

With Dunlop between jobs, Hendrik's future was uncertain, and with it the security of the Cesars family and its dependents. Having earned the disapproval of the Earl of Caledon and the military authorities, Dunlop's only option was to apply for home leave and await a new posting. Hendrik had to break the news to Anna Catharina that his master was returning to England, and that consequently he was out of a job. In all, the livelihoods of ten people, including Saartjie, depended upon Hendrik's employment.

Dunlop, Hendrik and Hendrik's brother Pieter must have been paying close attention to Saartjie, for it was at this point that they hatched an audacious plan that sealed her fate and secured their infamy as the villains who planned to build a fortune on the shaky foundations of one woman's buttocks. Looking for a means to secure a new livelihood, Dunlop persuaded the Cesars brothers that Saartjie had lucrative potential as a scientific curiosity in England. In an African context her build was unremarkable, but Dunlop believed that unfamiliarity could make her extraordinary in

European eyes; her image might be tailored to fulfil European fantasies about 'Hottentots'. The three men conspired to take Saartjie to London and option the rights to her exhibition on a contractual basis. They also planned to ship to London a giraffe skin, still a rarity in Britain. Inspired by the brisk trade in the ethnographically unusual fuelled by scientific imperialism, Dunlop and the Cesars brothers persuaded themselves that a pretty maidservant with notable buttocks and a spotty giraffe skin were a winning combination on which to stake their future.

As a military surgeon trained in Britain, Dunlop was well aware of the exploitative potential of live human exhibits. London had a thriving entertainment trade in human and scientific curiosities, and a person from an almost mythical African race might provide an exceptional draw for novelty-hungry European audiences. Hunter and tradesman Pieter Cesars was familiar with foreign explorers and botanists who paid good money for all manner of collectibles to ship back to Europe. Styling themselves men of science, many eighteenth-century ethnobotanical tourists and collectors such as Sir Joseph Banks called at the Cape Colony; others, like Carl Linnaeus, paid high prices from afar for its exotica.[15]

The first impediment to the plan to take Saartjie to England was that it was illegal. Under the Hottentot Proclamation, no Khoisan person was permitted to leave the colony without the direct permission of the Governor. The second problem was that Saartjie might prove resistant. She would need careful persuasion. It can only be imagined how Dunlop and the Cesars brothers presented this plan to her, and what promises, inducements and threats they made.

It is possible that Saartjie had captured Dunlop's sexual attentions. The impact of her allure on him was, after all, such that he believed he might make his fortune by peddling her as an African goddess of love. If he did take a fall for Saartjie, it was not an unusual pairing. Relationships between Khoisan women and white men of all classes had long been common at the Cape; The men deployed their racial and economic power to gratify their lusts and needs; the women, in some instances, gained economic benefits and, most precious of all, a white man usually offered the quickest route to freedom.[16] Equally, there were many recorded instances in which people, as they do, just lusted after each other or fell in love, irrespective of colour or creed.[17]

At the beginning of February 1810, Dunlop applied to the government requesting permission to take his male slave (unnamed in official documentation) with him to England as a servant-apprentice. Lord Caledon's secretary, Henry Alexander, authorised the request, providing that 'proper precautions are taken to secure the freedom of the Boy hereafter'.[18] Dunlop then applied to the Collector of Customs and Harbour Master Charles Blair requesting apprenticeship for this slave so that he could gain permission to travel. Blair, however, was away, not due to return until the end of March.

On 16 March, Dunlop wrote to the Governor's office and explained impatiently that 'being obliged to embark Monday next', he could wait no longer for certification from the Collector's office. Pressurised by Dunlop, Blair's deputy Thomas Ord confirmed in writing his understanding that before his departure Blair had given Dunlop his verbal approval, 'provided it meet the Governor's approbation'. 'Mr Ord,' Dunlop assured the Governor's office, pressing his advantage, 'will take care to get you a written certificate from Mr Blair the moment he returns.'[19]

Because Hendrik Cesars was not a white man, he too required a pass to leave the Cape colony. On 7 March, Hendrik went to the Governor's office armed with this intriguing letter from his master:

> The bearer Hendrik Cezar [sic], wishes to take the opportunity of going to England under my protection, and will be greatly obliged, if you will alter his pass or grant him a new one, which ever you think proper. He would have availed himself of going along with a friend of his, who went in the Wilhelmina but was prevented by sickness.[20]

The *Wilhelmina* was a British coasting schooner captained by Daniel Tack that plied cargoes of salt between Saldanha Bay on the west coast and Cape Town.[21] She had sailed from Table Bay on 4 March, three days before Cesars went to Lord Caledon's office to request permission to travel. The identity of Cesars's 'friend' is unknown, which makes Dunlop's letter ambiguous.

Piecing together the surviving fragments of evidence of the plan to smuggle Saartjie to England, it seems that she sailed the short local passage from Cape Town to Saldanha Bay on the *Wilhelmina* on 4 March, escorted by the trusted accomplice Pieter Cesars. She was lifted aboard ship by merchant seamen given the nod, and perhaps an extra ration of brandy for their connivance, by Captain Tack. As an officer and military surgeon, Dunlop and his entourage would take passage on a Navy ship, documented and cleared for departure at busy Table Bay, where passenger lists were officially logged. The Hottentot Proclamation made it impossible for Saartjie to travel legally with Dunlop from Cape Town without the authorisation of the governor, but, as every illegal slaver knew, merchant seamen were easier to bribe than military captains. Saldanha Bay was garrisoned, but remote. Navy transport ships took on cargo there, making it feasible to smuggle Saartjie aboard during the hectic bustle of winching and stowage. Additional travellers should, of course, have been added to the ship's log, but for the right price there was often a way to slip a stowaway aboard.

On 20 March Dunlop received permission from the Governor's office to depart from the Cape, 'together with his servant, on board the Diadem Transport commanded by William Davison [Master], bound to England'.[22] Approved by Lord Caledon, Dunlop's permission for departure was signed by the Governor's secretary, Henry Alexander.

Two days before, Hendrik Cesars set sail for England with his master, he and Anna Catharina visited the public notary's office to amend their will, making their daughter their universal heir and stipulating the release of their slave January of Mozambique from the estate on their death, bequeathing him the sum of 50 rix dollars (125 guilders). Hendrik marked his signature with a cross; Anna Catharina signed her name.[23]

The *Diadem* set sail on 1 April 1810,[24] captained by William Davison with an English crew of twenty-two sailors and five boys. A 455-tonne, 64-gun troop-ship,[25] she was on her way back for refitting at Chatham, the English dockyard where she had been built in 1782. The *Diadem* had spent 1809 plying between Simon's Bay and Table Bay provisioning the garrison and moving personnel. In service, she could hold a complement of up to 500 men.

Dunlop and Cesars' baggage included the huge, smelly giraffe skin, wrapped and rolled like a fermenting Turkish carpet in the cargo hold. The transport of the skin of a Camelopardalis, or what the poet Shelley called 'the spotted camelopard',[26] was still so unusual as to be newsworthy,[27] and Dunlop's precious, bulky cargo attracted interest as it was loaded aboard ship. This noisy, highly visible event was in stark contrast to the silent, muffled embarkation of a young black woman when the *Diadem* called in at Saldanha Bay.

Saartjie had no official permission to travel to England. By government decree, her papers would have had to have been presented to the ship's master, and her name entered in the log. Unfortunately the ship's musters for the *Diadem* from 14 December 1809 to 20 June 1810 are missing from Admiralty records.[28] It was wartime, and *HMS Diadem*, temporarily decommissioned pending her refurbishment, did not travel empty back to England. No doubt the *Diadem* would have taken cargo on board at Saldanha Bay, such as grain or salt, and, amid the bustle, a female stowaway.

Thus Saartjie's roguish managers succeeded in spiriting her out of the Cape Colony. Orphaned and unprotected, bereft of a mother's counsel or of older women to offer cautionary tales, Saartjie was vulnerable to coercion and the promises made to her by Dunlop and

Hendrik Cesars. Economically dependent, she was not in a position to negotiate. With hindsight it is easy to see that Saartjie was lured across the world to her doom. However, the promise of new adventure offered some palliative solace for her losses, trauma and miseries. What was left to keep Saartjie in Cape Town? It is not hard to see how she was persuaded to exchange interminable domestic servitude for the enticements of a regular wage, the hope of greater freedom in England, and even the possibility of fame and fortune. Saartjie later said that Dunlop had 'promised to send her back rich.'[29] It is clear that she expected to return home; Dunlop and Cesars guaranteed to send her back to Cape Town after a period of six years in England, with 'the money belonging to her'[30] and at their expense.[31]

By means of a short voyage on the *Wilhelmina* from Cape Town to Saldanha Bay, from where the *Diadem* carried her off to England, Saartjie was smuggled from South Africa. As the *Wilhelmina* sailed away from Cape Town, it is unlikely that Saartjie looked at Table Mountain with any wistfulness. She was not free, but she was freer than many, and any freedom was better than none. Her understandable trepidation at embarking clandestinely, and with an all-male crew, might have been mingled with a sense of naive expectation. She was young, resilient and seemed adventurous. She knew she was not travelling afar to remain just a domestic servant; no one got rich from that. Was she looking forward to being wealthy, as Dunlop and Cesars had promised? Was she curious about what it meant to be starting a new life as a representative of her people, or utterly mystified by the whole proposition?

The Cape peninsula is best surveyed from the lofty top of the Adamastor like Table Mountain.[32] On a sun-drenched, cloudless day, the arc of the horizon is seemingly illimitable, as if the eye were falling off the edge of the world, and the elated, uncertain heart impelled to follow its leap. Sky and ocean shift through the spectrum of colours of hope and yearning, from dazzling cerulean blue to violet, indigo and muted silver-grey.

Viewed from the vantage point of the mountain, the ship would have looked like a toy. Yet for earthbound Saartjie, sailing beneath the water-line beyond her farthest horizons must have been an experience filled with mystery, physical discomfort and fear. In this great, expansive seascape, Saartjie's world contracted to wind and sails, permanently damp and salty clothes, bitter food, a tiny scrap of sleeping space beneath a hammock – and no clear picture of what lay ahead.

5

VENUS RISING

The Venus of ancient mythology, goddess of love and desire, rose naked from the foaming sea and stepped ashore onto a small island where grass and flowers sprang from the soil wherever she trod. The Seasons hastened to clothe and adorn her. The Hottentot Venus, however, arrived in England an illicit, precariously positioned immigrant. The *Diadem* made landfall at Plymouth in May 1810.[1] Saartjie stepped ashore wearing sea-damp servant's smocking, stiff with salt from the long voyage, and inadequate rawhide shoes. Her few personal possessions included her sheepskin kaross, her musical instruments and her tortoiseshell pendant.

While Saartjie may have been wishing for dry, warm clothes and stronger shoes, Dunlop and Hendrik Cesars were preoccupied with making arrangements to transport both the giraffe skin and their trunks containing the accessories with which they would array her as a Hottentot Venus. As shown in Saartjie's earliest publicity images, this *authentica*, probably garnered by Pieter Cesars on his trading trips, included ivory bracelets, ostrich-shell necklaces, wood and bone bead belts, anklets, earrings, an elaborate head-band, and an imposing and intricately wrought bridal necklace. There were also ostrich feathers, an assortment of pipes, and a bushbuck apron of the design traditionally worn by rural women to cover their genitals for modesty.

Huddled together on unsteady land-legs awaiting the first stagecoach to London, the bluff military surgeon and his sea-dazed companions must have resembled nothing so much as a travelling showman with his troupe of curiosi-ties, hung about by unusual musical instruments, sea-chests and the outsized, noisome giraffe skin.

As Saartjie entered the mighty wilderness of London by stage coach that spring of 1810, perhaps her senses were overwhelmed by the whirl and uproar of its tumultuous streets, smelling of dung and smoke. Insignificant and anonymous as she entered its vortex, Saartjie could little imagine that within a few months she would be singled out as the talk of Europe's biggest metropolis.

Dunlop, still on full officer's pay, took lodgings for the entourage on York Street, off St James's Square, and hired an additional black manservant. York Street, St James's Square, Pall Mall, St James's Street, Piccadilly and Bond Street were the main arteries of the golden square mile where the idle rich danced, gambled, gossiped and shopped their way through the final year of the reign of George III. A short distance away at Westminster, Parliament was debating the success of the Duke of Wellington's campaign to hold Portugal against the French.

St James's Palace was larger than any building Saartjie had ever seen, and Whitehall was still startlingly white, as yet untarnished by coal-dust. Saartjie was among the very first people to experience the artificial illumination of central London; the city's experiment with newfangled gas street-lighting provided 'a vivid white . . . brilliant light'[2] and gave the streets of Piccadilly by night the luminosity of a dream.

Saartjie heard the unfamiliar, flat-vowelled voices of Londoners. She saw African and Indian men in European suits; white women in brightly coloured and precariously balanced silk turbans, ostrich plumes and Indian shawls; children of all races in rags; and tripe stalls festooned with slick entrails, penny a cup.

St James's Square had been London's most fashionable district since the Restoration. Saartjie had illustrious neighbours in Piccadilly, many of whom she met or who paid to see her. Beau Brummell and Tom Sheridan, compulsive gamblers at Watier's Club, were among her future audience. Tom Sheridan's father, the politician and playwright Richard Brinsley Sheridan, MP for Ilchester, would also encounter The Hottentot Venus. Lord Grenville, whose name was shortly to be publicly linked with Saartjie's, lived nearby in Cleveland Square. Grenville's political pedigree included Speaker of the House, Secretary of State for Foreign Affairs and First Lord of the Treasury. He was a leading campaigner against slavery, worked alongside Charles James Fox, leader of the liberal Whig party, and carried the resolutions in favour of abolition in June 1806. Other denizens of Piccadilly included Mrs Coutts, widow of the successful banker, and Lord Palmerston, Earl of Elgin, who kept his expropriated marbles at Gloucester House until Parliament resolved they should be moved to the British Museum.

Piccadilly's reputation as a magnet for artists had been established in the eighteenth century; John Gay, William Hogarth, Alexander Pope, Jonathan Swift and George Frideric Handel all immortalised the area in their works, and enjoyed the hospitality of their patrons in its grand houses.

Whig leaders frequented Piccadilly, and Sir Francis Burdett, known to all as 'Old Glory', lived at No. 80. Shortly after her arrival, Saartjie found herself in the midst of a popular uprising. On 18 June, Burdett's denunciation of Parliamentary corruption resulted in the order for his committal to the Tower of London. Indignant protestors flocked to Piccadilly to resist his arrest. The military were called in, the Riot Act read, windows smashed, barricades erected and a candlelit night vigil kept by the protestors. After three days of siege, several deaths and injuries, the Sergeant at Arms stormed Burdett's house and he was taken into custody. Simultaneously, a tumultuous thunderstorm broke over central London, flooding the streets and channelling attention away from the political unrest. The storm was, some historians claimed, the only thing that saved London from a mass uprising against its rotten rulers.[3]

Late Georgian Piccadilly was also the epicentre of science and showmanship. Sir Joseph Banks, who became famous as the botanist on Captain Cook's first voyage to Australia in 1768, presided over London's Royal Society at Somerset House nearby, in the Strand. Enlightenment scientists, medics, naturalists and explorers saw themselves as quite distinct from the showmen, crackpots and quacks who plied their entertainments day in and day out around Piccadilly, but in the public mind they were generally regarded as one and the same. Banks strove to convince the government that serious scientific research was an economic and political necessity for imperial expansion, but his nickname, 'Botanic Macaroni', illustrates the irreverence with which he was popularly regarded. The public harboured the suspicion that Banks was little more than a sexual tourist whose libertine obsessions compelled him to laughable erotic allusion, *even* when categorising plants.[4]

Many of the specimens Banks collected on that South Seas expedition were displayed in Bullock's Liverpool Museum at 22 Piccadilly, described at the beginning of 1810 by *Bell's Weekly Messenger* as 'the most fashionable place of amusement in London'.[5] The Liverpool Museum was the creation of traveller and naturalist William Bullock, a close friend of Banks, who had purchased many curiosities from Cook's voyages.

In August, while Saartjie was still adjusting to English beer and mutton pies, Dunlop approached London's most successful museum master with a commercial proposition. He offered to sell Bullock his 'camel-opard skin of great beauty and considerable value',[6] brought recently from the Cape of Good Hope. Dunlop also revealed that he was, as Bullock put it, 'in possession of a Hottentot Woman',[7] who was available to be contracted for exhibition for two years. After this period, Dunlop explained, he 'was under an engagement to return her to the Cape of Good Hope'.[8] Dunlop emphasised 'the extraordinary shape and make of the woman',[9] stressing her value as 'an object of great curiosity,[10] and arguing that she 'would make the fortune of any person by exhibiting her (for the said two years) to the public'.[11] Suspiciously, this two-year period contradicted

Saartjie's later claim that her contract was for six years.[12]

Liverpudlian Bullock had already made his fortune. Starting as a jeweller-silversmith, the young entrepreneur collected rare specimens of natural history from the captains and crews of ships returning to the port, chiefly from James Cook.[13] Bullock opened his first exhibition of diverse natural and artificial curiosities in Liverpool in 1795. In 1809 he moved Bullock's Liverpool Museum to London, where, within a month of opening, it became the city's most successful attraction. By June the following year a record 80,000 people had entered the doors, and a permanent queue stretched outside.

Bullock's catalogue boasted that his exhibition, in which he had invested a staggering 22,000 pounds, included 'upwards of 7000 Natural and Foreign Curiosities, antiquities, and productions of the fine arts'.[14] He was the first English museum director to organise his specimens according to their habitat groups, and to display his objects with a choreographer's care for posture and appropriate environment.[15] Twenty-two Piccadilly was a great emporium of objects and dead animals. Bullock's organised havoc of cross-cultural objects varied hugely in value and usefulness; some were priceless, others worthless. Above all, his collection exemplified the hoarding instincts of imperialism.

Bullock admired Dunlop's giraffe skin, beautifully spotted with dark brown on a cream-coloured ground. Once stuffed, it would be nearly twice the height of a full-grown elephant and provide a newsworthy addition to his famous Artificial Forest, the centrepiece of the museum.[16] After two meetings, the men agreed terms on the skin. However, Bullock flatly rejected Dunlop's distasteful proposal to sell him the right to exhibit the 'Hottentot Woman', declaring that 'such an exhibition would not meet the countenance of the public'.[17] He was a museum director, not the keeper of a freak show.[18]

Bullock did not, as yet, exhibit live human curiosities. A member of a host of learned societies, including the Horticultural, Geological and Wernerian, the well-connected Bullock regarded himself as a respectable businessman. Significantly, just as Dunlop approached him offering Saartjie's contract, Bullock was in the process of trying to get himself elected a Fellow of the Linnean Society. Although he eventually succeeded, his proposal as a candidate caused protest among some of the society's more snobbish members, who regarded his commercial success as vulgar. William Elford Leach wrote to the Fellows, entreating them

> . . . if they are friends to Science and Enemies to Quackery to attend the Linnean Meeting on Tuesday next Nov. 6th for the purpose of blackballing Mr Bullock . . . who by puffs with which he daily fills the newspapers is likely to bring that hitherto respectable body into disrepute.[19]

Bullock also moved in abolitionist circles and was wary of the possibility that Saartjie, a member of a subject nation, might have been brought to England against her will. He felt a genuine ethical objection to Dunlop's proposal, but it was also the case that his involvement in her exhibition might scupper his entry to the Linnean Society and dent his carefully cultivated propriety.

Twelve years later, in 1825, Bullock exhibited an entire

living family of Laplanders in Piccadilly, from which it seems that he did not object *tout court* to putting humans on display as live specimens. Nor dead ones. In 1813 he planned to take Oliver Cromwell's severed head on a tour around England. The then Prime Minister, Lord Liverpool, was the only person able to dissuade him from this enterprise.[20]

Master and servant's dreams of quick riches foundered, but, notably, Dunlop did not try to solve the problem by selling Saartjie's performance rights to one of London's many established freak-show impresarios.[21] With no reputable alternative exhibitors to approach, Dunlop and Cesars determined to manage Saartjie's exhibition themselves.

Using money realised from the giraffe skin, they set about in search of a suitable venue, began to plan their advertising and considered the development of Saartjie's show. Dunlop and Cesars's attitude was that Saartjie offered a ready-made attraction, but she needed to do more than just shift, pout and wiggle around a stage to entice jaded London audiences to part with the 2-shilling ticket price. Here, her musical skills and exhilarating, misspent evenings in the Cape taverns came into play. Saartjie had brought with her her *ramkie* and a bowed lute.[22] Dunlop and Cesars importuned her to be ready to perform her repertoire of folk-songs in Afrikaans and Khoi. She would also be required to dance – 'in the manner of her country'.[23] The Hottentot Venus exhibition would open for four hours, six days a week, placing a heavy demand on Saartjie who would need the ingenuity to devise an engaging routine and the stamina to repeat it throughout the long afternoon shows.

Location was critical. Dunlop and Cesars reasoned, correctly, that a venue near the Liverpool Museum might pick up business from the crowds pressing to see Bullock's novelties. They secured 225 Piccadilly, on the north side of the thoroughfare, diagonally across from the museum.

Piccadilly was the heart of London's brisk trade in natural and artificial human freaks, curiosities, 'wonders' and popular entertainments. A *Punch* cartoon entitled 'Deformito-mania' captures the district's nature as the centre of the amusement trade, with its exhibitionist excess of exaggeration and theatrical expostulation. The cartoon shows riotous hordes of well-heeled, silk-top-hatted men and fashionably dressed, bonneted women crowding through the doors of the 'Hall of Wonder', whose street-front is plastered with the sensation-alist sign 'THIS IS THE NE PLUS ULTRA OF HIDEOUSNESS, ACKNOWLEDGED SUCH BY THE PRESS!' pasted next to the 'Hall of Ugliness', which in turn

THE DEFORMITO-MANIA.

promises 'THE GREATEST DEFORMITY IN THE WORLD WITHIN: NO CONNECTION WITH DEFORMITY NEXT DOOR', and, next door, 'BY FAR THE UGLIEST BIPED IS HERE, ONE SHILLING'.[24]

The entertainment trade in human deformities specialised in live exhibits. Many acts were straightforward exploitations of human variation and disease for which there was not as yet any medical remedy. Siamese twins and albino children (advertised as 'White Negroes') were paraded at street fairs throughout the eighteenth century. In June 1810, a West Indian child advertised as 'The Piebald Boy' was put on show in the Strand. Those who suspected he was painted were invited to scratch or rub him on the promise that they would soon find out that he was genuinely mottled.[25] Other popular freak shows in the area included 'The Fasting Woman of Tetbury'; the 50 stone Daniel Lambert, or Fat Dan, the fattest man who ever lived; the Frenchman Claude Ambroise Seurat, 'The Living Skeleton', conversely the thinnest; and 19½-inch Caroline Crachami, the miniature 'Sicilian Fairy'.[26]

The concept of a Hottentot Venus fitted well with the Piccadilly tradition of goddesses, sea marvels and other mythical creatures which had attached themselves to the area from its earliest days. The famous Water-Theatre of the ingenious Mr Winstanley (boxes 2 shillings) offered gods and goddesses, nymphs, mermaids, satyrs and later even flying dragons, 'their mouths filled with fire, water, and perfumes',[27] all culminating in a dramatic 'sea-triumph'[28] tableau. This finale was choreographed around a large barrel of liquor broken into pieces in front of the thirsty spectators, who drank its contents, thus ensuring a regularly packed house. At 225 Piccadilly, Saartjie would therefore be exhibited in the acknowledged homeland of theatrical curiosities from beneath and across the ocean.

Inspired by Bullock's carefully orchestrated settings for his exhibits, Dunlop and Cesars got to work on dressing the stage at 225 Piccadilly in a manner that would invoke a sense of Africa. They commissioned the painting of wooden flats depicting African pastoral landscapes and flora. These framed the centrepiece of the set, a grass hut signifying Saartjie's home. For the exhibition of a human curiosity at the beginning of the nineteenth century, it was a lot of scenery. The fabulously successful Giant O'Brien, for example, had only a stool for his set.[29]

Saartjie's Venus costume was critical to the success of the show. Above all, it was necessary to create the illusion of her semi-nakedness. Her ensemble, though not strictly typical of a Khoisan woman 'in her natural state, was at any rate suggestive of South Africa'.[30] Londoners had long been familiar with rumours about the extraordinary shape of Hottentot women, but the opportunity to see such a woman in the flesh was a novelty. As with a mermaid or a monster, this unfamiliarity put Saartjie in the category of a wonder whose existence needed to be seen to be believed.

Dunlop and Cesars wanted to demonstrate that Saartjie's bottom, the source of her potential fame, was a bona fide physiological anomaly, and to hint at the legendary extended labia attributed to Khoisan women by the uncorroborated claims of numerous European travellers to the Cape. The accessories brought from Cape Town provided the adornment for Saartjie's Venus costume, arranged in composite layers over her fleshings, a tailor-made one-piece body-stocking, or leotard, fashioned from a figure-hugging fabric of silk and cotton. Saartjie was measured and pinned for this bespoke silken garment, designed to make her appear as nature made her. To be realistic, it needed to fit as snugly as a second skin. Fostering the fallacy of Saartjie's bared flesh, all the publicity images concealed the seams, buttons and hooks that held the fleshings tightly in place, making it cling to every contour of her body. To hide the seams and conceal the places where this garment ended at her neck, hands and ankles, Saartjie arranged abundant jewellery and adornments. A torrent of ostrich-shell and bead necklaces cascaded in shiny strings from her décolletage. Jangling cuffs of five bracelets, possibly ivory, hung from each of her wrists, and ostrich-feather anklets studded with beads brushed her slippered feet.

Slung about with necklaces, belts and ostrich plumes, Saartjie's outer garment was effectively a skimpy mesh of beads and feathers. A rectangular apron, embroidered and edged with pearly beading, was placed strategically above her pubic bone – her Mound of Venus. From underneath this camouflage hung pendants of hide cured to a malleable buttery softness, each tapering into a rippling striped cord finished with ostrich-feather tassels, like a row of silken bell-pulls, brushing the bows on Saartjie's slippers. It was an elaborate, exaggerated female codpiece of dramatic size. The effect of its soft folds, fur fringes and pendulous extensions was to imply that its purpose was to modestly conceal her elongated labia.

The complexity of this apparel, with its hard-to-reach back fastenings, meant that Saartjie needed help dressing. She said that she had 'two Black Boys to wait upon her' at York Street, and explained that either Dunlop or Cesars assisted her 'in the morning when she is nearly completely attired, for the purposes of fastening the Ribbon around her waist'.[31] Saartjie used grease paint, kohl, powder, combs and oil to make up her face and hair.

There is no written record of the origin of Saartjie's Venus soubriquet. It was a Classical reference, of course. But, more than that, Venus was simply a synonym for sex. In the same period, 'Hottentot' signified all that was other: strange, disturbing, culturally alien, sexually deviant and excessive. United, the words Hottentot and Venus carried a potent force. They coupled Eros with notions of ugliness, desire with degradation, licence with taboo, and transcendent goddess with carnal beast; they articulated the alarming siren allure of feminine concupiscence – Aristotle's fascinating, terrifying *animal avidum generandi*, the beast greedy for generation.[32] These high-falutin Latin tags were not, however, the words the ballad-criers used to advertise Saartjie's putatively extraordinary pudenda to passers-by.

On Wednesday, 12th September, Sir Joseph Banks, along with other members of London's social élite and intelligentsia,[33] received his invitation to attend the exclusive preview of The Hottentot Venus on the following Monday. On Thursday, 20 September, advertisements announcing the public opening of the exhibition appeared in the *Morning Herald* and *Morning Post*. Written by Dunlop, these advertisements took care to cast Cesars – 'a native of the Cape' – in the role of Saartjie's *foreign* manager.

Saartjie first performed in front of a paying public audience at lunchtime on Monday 24 September. What went through her mind, what emotions and physical sensations did she experience that day exposed in her new, unfamiliar costume? Uncertainty, bemusement, anxiety, the adrenalin rush of fear? For the first time, Saartjie was raised above those around her, an entirely new perspective.

The exhibition room glowed with torches, candles and oil lamps, illuminating the small stage at one end, with its centre-piece grass hut and painted flats uplit by reflectors contrived from mirrors and coloured water. At the back of the stage was a curtained recess where Saartjie waited as the room filled with punters, shuffling with curiosity and expectation.

Like other human curiosities, freak acts and floor shows, the Hottentot Venus exhibition was a loosely choreographed routine. It opened with Saartjie emerging from the hut at the summons of Cesars.[34] She took up a downstage position, struck up a song on her *ramkie*, and began to sing and dance. Observers remarked that she had 'a fairly good ear'[35] and sang pleasingly but that playing and dancing were her stronger talents. She strummed, she hummed, she strutted and wriggled and sashayed and sang.[36] Saartjie sang folk and popular songs in Khoi, Afrikaans and English, some to tunes easily recognisable to her London audience, although Dunlop and Cesars preferred her to sing traditional folk-songs in order to emphasise her strangeness and authenticity. People heard different things in Saartjie's music. Some believed they heard the call of home and the familiar, some the humour and wit of a playful, disdainful courtesan. Others heard something reckless, innocent and bold: the tragic keynotes of a young, isolated woman adrift in a strange country far from the land of her birth.

Of all the sounds that defined Saartjie, her *ramkie* was the most distinguishing. In the evolution of this African guitar is compressed the diversity of 600 years of South African history. Descended from the original Khoi gourd and nut instruments, the *ramkie* merged, through trade routes, colonisation and slavery, with influences from Portugal and the East, mainly India and Malaysia, and later developed into the tin-can guitar. By the early nineteenth century, its arpeggios denoted African, Asian, Arab and Western harmonies; this music was a direct antecedent to the blues.

Physicality has its own language: rhythms, secret chords, minor falls and major lifts. As instantly became evident from sensational responses to her performance, Saartjie was both a subtle and an imposing artist of the bodily form. Press descriptions offered elusive glimpses of her personality: wry humour, anger, sensual composure, deft movement, refusal, stoicism, confrontation – all were essential to her arsenal of engagement.

Almost overnight, London was overtaken by Saartjie-mania. She instantly captured the public imagination. After centuries of fabulous myths and traveller's tall tales, London finally had a real, live, all-singing, all-dancing Hottentot Venus who appeared to confirm them. Saartjie became London's most popular novelty. In the course of just one week, she went from being an anonymous, recently arrived illegal immigrant to being one of the city's most talked-about women, her image ubiquitous, her name swapped with wide-eyed murmurs between gossiping socialites and bawled by newsboys on the streets.

There was an excited outpouring of 'SARTJEE'-themed popular poesy, ballads, broadsheet caricatures, articles and printed satires. Her image proliferated, seemingly reproduced everywhere, on brightly coloured posters pasted in shop windows, on penny prints held aloft by street sellers and city criers, the human tabloids who shouted 'SARTJEE' and 'HOTTENTOT' throughout the metropolis.

Every day except Sundays, Saartjie also gave exclusive evening private views, restricted to parties of twelve, which had to be booked twenty-four hours in advance. Night and day, Saartjie was subject, object, be-all and obsessively ogled-at end-all of the show. The success of The Hottentot Venus depended upon a contradiction: Saartjie needed to be perceived as a unique novelty whilst typifying the image of the Hottentot. Africans in England were no longer of them-selves a remarkable curiosity.[37] The permanent black population of Britain at the beginning of the nineteenth century was about 20,000,[38] with numbers steadily rising following abolition in 1807. British cities were already multi-ethnic.

To promote her novelty, Saartjie's managers focused on accentuating her difference. They aimed to persuade audiences that The Hottentot Venus had a bottom unequalled by any to be seen in London. A verse published in the *Morning Herald* demonstrates how the media responded:

> Though Venus, of old,
> By records, we're told,
> Excited the praise of mankind;
> Our Hottentot, still,
> Let her die when she will,
> Will not leave her equal *behind*.[39]

Bottoms were big in Georgian England. From low to high culture of all forms, Britain was a nation obsessed by buttocks, bums, arses, posteriors, derrières and every possible metaphor, joke or pun that could be squeezed from this fundamental cultural obsession. From the front parlour to Parliament, from prostitution to pornography, Georgian England both exuberantly celebrated, and earnestly deplored, excess, grossness, extreme bawdiness and the uncontainable. Much of Saartjie's success was a result of a simple phenomenon: with her shimmying, voluptuous bottom, she perfectly captured the counter-zeitgeist of late Georgian Britain.

Handbills and poster advertisements promoted The Hottentot Venus as a natural wonder, a new 'specimen' of a little-known tribe whose buttocks and suggestively fringed labial Venus apron shaped her mystery. To some degree this was of course marketing hokum, as Khoisan people had been visiting London, and attracting considerable public attention, since the seventeenth century. None of them, however, had been suggestively clad, generously endowed proto-showgirls. The exaggerated claims made about Saartjie's 'tribal' history were an accepted convention of Piccadilly showmanship. The by now familiar presence of black Londoners meant that the myth of the noble savage was already as tarnished as the notion that the capital's proletarian classes were naive urban savages who believed in gods and monsters. Whatever Dunlop's pretensions to provide scientific and cultural illumination to the literati, Saartjie was a sexpot Venus who showed her legs.[40] The use of the Venus soubriquet was a clever marketing technique offering audiences the opportunity to see a putatively naked African goddess. The key to her popularity was not in the scale of her physical endowments, however, but in her music, in the way she moved and in her skills as an entertainer. Without these, London would have tired of her much sooner. Saartjie must have wondered what the audience was really coming to see. Maybe they would be happy if she just stood on stage without playing and shook her body from her head to her toes all afternoon while they gazed at her in jaw-dropping amazement. Playing to white men looking up at her with glinting animal eyes, surrounded by them, she surely came to understand their desires, perhaps better than she understood her own.[41]

Saartjie became the most famous theatrical attraction in Piccadilly in the transition between two distinct historical moments in English racial attitudes. She arrived towards the end of the era when sentimental primitivism held sway and at the beginning of the rise of the new pseudo-science of ethnology, in which human beings became living specimens.[42] Ethnology went hand in white cotton glove and khaki pith-helmet with imperialism, the economic exploitation of Africa and the emergence of scientific racism. Saartjie's arrival in London coincided with a new era of expansion into the African interior, feminised by its would-be British colonisers as a continent ripe for conquest. Dovetailing with this was the fact that African otherness, with its implications of the alien and strange, had an appeal long exploited by theatrical and popular entertainments. The Hottentot Venus arose in London as the very apotheosis of Europe's invented Africa, the dark continent of feminised impenetrability and crude potency.

The metropolitan élite soon began to summon Saartjie to their grand houses as a novelty act to entertain dinner and party guests. One of her most memorable private audiences was with the ultimate Regency rake William, the 4th Duke of Queensbury; he was known as 'Old Q', famed celebrity millionaire, amateur jockey, and debauched voluptuary. Debauchery and indiscriminate lovemaking served Queensbury well. He expired in bed on 23 December 1810 at the age of eighty-six, surrounded by seventy love letters from as many women, crying 'Billet doux!' with his last breath.

A month before he died, Old Q invited Saartjie to a dinner party at his lavish mansion at 138 and 139 Piccadilly, where he was said to bathe daily in a silver bath filled with milk. Queensbury was the last of the nobility to keep running footmen, one of whom was sent to 225 Piccadilly to instruct the management that The Hottentot Venus was required for an audience with the Duke, who sent a sedan chair to collect her. The *Morning Herald* reported:

> A few evenings since, the *Hottentot Venus* paid a chair visit to a venerable Duke, who still preserves a taste for CHOICE things. After a microscopic inspection of her prominent beauties, she danced . . . to the exquisite satisfaction of his Grace, and a select party of *Amateurs* of natural productions.[43]

The press revealed that Saartjie 'danced an African fandango in a style of true savage simplicity', and then bathed in Old Q's silver tub, her bottom described as 'the tempting crust of a well rasped roll floating in a tureen of savoury soup'.[44] The image was a bawdy play on the proverbial racist conceit that it was impossible 'to wash the Ethiop white'.[45]

Lord Grenville, Sir Joseph Banks and the picturesque poet R. P. Knight attended, prompting the *Satirist* to a spoof.

Queensbury, the parody proposed, formed a committee to ascertain whether or not The Hottentot Venus had, as rumoured, an ancestral connection to the house of Buckingham, and could therefore be claimed as a direct relative of the big-bottomed Lord Grenville. Given his political position, Lord Grenville's broad flanks were a gift to the press.

By the winter of 1810, it was evident that George III would soon leave the throne. Pundits believed that when the Prince Regent succeeded his father, he would dissolve Parliament and invite Lord Grenville and his Whig coalition to take over. To all of England, Grenville and his political cohort had been known as the broad bottoms since the short-lived Grenville–Fox coalition of 1806, the so-called 'Ministry of all the Talents'. Saartjie's rise to fame coincided with the press's preoccupation with the fate of the broad bottomites who, it was believed, would soon be running Parliament once again. The convergence of Lord Grenville's broad bottom with that of The Hottentot Venus was a journalist's dream, and a ceaseless outpouring of prose caricature and cartoons was the result. The obsession with Saartjie's posterior, posterity, broad-bottomedness and endless punning on rear ends, rumps, fundaments and fat arses became explicitly tied to the most pressing and topical political issues concerning the decline of King George, the rise of the Regency, and which rumps would take over government. Rumps also had dangerously republican connotations from the 1649–53 Rump Parliament.

In this context, Saartjie's visit to the insatiable Queensbury, a close friend of Lord Grenville, set the scene for fulsome satire. According to the *Satirist*, when they entered his parlour, Old Q informed his illustrious guests

that Saartjie was about to have a milk bath in his famous
tub, and that he had 'offered to officiate at the ablutionary
rites'. In the narrator's voyeuristic fantasy, Saartjie slips into
the tub in a posture of submission, to the Duke's delight:

> So floated the distinguishing feature of the interesting Hottentot
> in the lacteal bath, the rest of her body being completely
> immersed, so gazed, with anxious eye his grace of Queensbury.
> Having tired her fine form with studious and tender care, he
> informed his valet that the milkman might now have the milk
> for his customers, and handed her to the parlour.[46]

Sir Joseph Banks then took Saartjie's measurements with
his 'newly invented instrument called a "*gloutometer*", with
which, he claimed, he would quickly discover if there were
any affinity between the Grenville and the Hottentot protuberances'.[47] Queensbury, hovering lecherously, suggested
that a more reliable comparison might be made by inviting
some of Lord Grenville's big-bottomed female relations for
inspection. Banks's ethnographic bottom-measuring experiment concluded, Queensbury insisted that Saartjie
remain 'beneath his hospitable roof till next morning. She
politely acceded to his request, and, of course, felt highly
gratified by his grace's kind attentions'.[48]

Speculations on Saartjie's impressions of London became
a particularly favoured subject for satire. A host of editors
and journalists across broadsheets, journals and monthly
circulars took the opportunity to poke fun at native English
culture through the eyes of this naive South African foreigner.
Far off the geographical mark, however, the satires always
rendered Saartjie's voice in cod Anglo-Jamaican patois.

'De Hottentot Fenus' commented, with sparkling wit and trenchant observation, on newsworthy matters, such as the dispute over the rising cost of bread due to the war with Napoleon's empire. Sometimes couched within these topicalities were scenes which gained their humorous force by playing on Saartjie's reputation for forthright behaviour and quick temper. The *Morning Post*, for instance, ran a spoof letter from 'De Hottentot Fenus To De Gret Lord Grinwell, who desire her to write him what she tink of dis country'.[49] In it, Venus is visited by a politician 'from debate shop' who 'den introduce beauty from Forum', but Venus is unimpressed:

I laugh at her, she so dam frightful. He den say he want me speak with her, at debate shop; I say me no go where such a set. Den he grin, *Beauty* frown, me no care. Debate man repeat nonsense, he want me speak; I laugh louder – he fool, may go Newgate. I turn *back* on him, and *send him out of room*. Beauty faint; dat very common, she used to it. I give slap of face; she come back, get up, and say, 'I rise blow you up, you dam *Hot*tentot.' I give her another slap; she ran out, and called Jack. Her leave an old wig behind, and little beggarly bag; cosmetics in it and little cards – dem me told tickets of *pawn man*. Dat very bad; oh fie! she sad one.[50]

For publicity, Dunlop and Cesars arranged for Saartjie to take regular Sunday carriage rides around central London.[51] From her carriage Saartjie could see the lime trees in St James's Park, their summer foliage bottle-green under a pale, diffuse sheepskin sky. Those who saw Venus's coach pass – street sellers, rag-and-bone men, the rushing or loitering crowd, – pressed forward to catch a look at the now-famous African icon. From amid the cacophony, Saartjie would have heard her Anglicised name, Sartjee, belted out in the sensational verses of the ballad-criers. On shop-fronts, street corners and newspaper stalls she saw posters bearing the image of her stage self, reflected back at her, vivid with aquatint, larger than life. Was that really supposed to be her, that woman standing in exaggerated profile, breasts and buttocks aloft, dressed like a tribal bride, looking determinedly ahead, pipe in her mouth, smoke curling upwards?

6

FREEWOMAN OR SLAVE?

A fortnight into her exhibition, Saartjie caught flu. London was frenetic with talk about The Hottentot Venus; the name SAARTJEE could be seen and heard from Seven Dials to St Paul's. It was not a good time to be sick. There was no question of Cesars and Dunlop jeopardising their success. Their Venus would play on.

Saartjie sniffed and sneezed her way through the repetitive performances with increasingly aching limbs. One long, wet afternoon, matters came to a head when a spectator challenged Cesars about her ill health. Cesars retorted that she 'was always sulky when company was there',[1] but Saartjie pointed to her throat and knees 'as if she felt pain in both, pleading with tears that he would not force her compliance'.[2] Unmoved, Cesars brandished his bamboo walking-stick and told her to stop sulking and get on with it; as a witness remarked, 'she saw it, knew its power, and, though ill, delayed no longer.'[3] It was a pathetic tableau, charged with the menace of domestic violence which, many believed, was replicated in the off-stage relationship between showgirl and manager.

While Saartjie played her guitar, 'a gentleman chanced to laugh'[4] insultingly at her. Roused by 'sickness, servitude'[5] and fury, she set about the man and 'endeavoured to strike him with the musical instrument'.[6] Cesars capitalised on the drama, declaring his Venus 'wild as a beast'.[7] Many of the spectators were all too willing to agree.[8]

This episode set the pattern for many similar instances of Saartjie's publicly exhibited discontent. She protested — noisily, physically, viscerally — against the unscrupulous lucksters who exploited her, and against offensive punters. The heightened element of personal drama in this dynamic of threat and grudging submission added an intense atmosphere of kinetic, unsettling energy. The show reinforced the expected relationship between white master and black slave, and audiences barely questioned its authenticity. Yet it was an age of popular entertainments, human freak shows and two-a-penny illusions. Saartjie was perceived as a traditionally dressed, temperamentally unpredictable 'native from the African interior', and Cesars was readily believed to be one of those devilish Boers so recently routed by the moral might of the abolitionist British.

As a result of her forceful public displays of displeasure, Saartjie attracted the attention of anti-slavery campaigners. A letter to the editor of the *Examiner* on Sunday, 21 October, written by the abolitionist Zachary Macaulay, protested:

> To a contemplative and feeling man few things are so painful as to behold the degradation of his species: under whatever disguise the spectacle may be veiled, whether as an object of science or natural research, it is nevertheless a disgusting, afflictive and mortifying sight.[9]

It is to Saartjie's great credit that the depth of her sighs and intractable sullenness became as legendary as her omnipotent buttocks. A grumpy Venus, she made an art of petulance. 'By her gestures and sighs she seemed evidently depressed, and evinced a sullen reluctance to obey the commands of her keeper,'[10] chafed the *Sporting Magazine*, likening Cesars to a slave-owner, circus ring-master or animal tamer. In a final image of animal debasement, it suggested that Saartjie was 'shewn like a chained beast'.[11] This simile, used to gain public sympathy for her plight, created the myth that she performed chained and in a cage. Although many women have appeared both before and since on leashes, chained or in cages, both legally enslaved and commercially enslaved for purposes of popular entertainment, Saartjie was not one of them.

Saartjie's plight, and the question of her consent, were about to make national headlines. Saartjie was caught in the contradictions of Enlightenment redefinitions of human freedom. In legal terms, abolition made the difference between slavery and servitude a question of self-possession, not escape from economic poverty. But for Saartjie, there were also economic advantages to be gained.

'No nation in Europe . . . has . . . plunged so deeply into this guilt as Great Britain,' said William Pitt the Younger of the slave trade in the House of Commons in 1792. In 1803 Henry Brougham reminded Parliament that 'we have been the chief trader, I mean the ringleaders in the crime.'[12] Abolitionism in England, which had its roots in republican revolutionary politics, was by the early nineteenth century entangled with Christian notions of responsibility, exculpation from guilt, the quest for redemption and free-market capitalist philanthropy.

Lord Grenville opposed slavery from the first Commons debate on the trade in 1789, the year of Saartjie's birth. Succeeding Pitt, Prime Minister Lord Grenville, with Foreign Secretary Charles James Fox, moved resolutions for abolition in both houses in June 1806. Lord Chancellor Thomas Erskine changed his mind in favour, and, fifteen years after William Wilberforce introduced the first abolitionist motion into Parliament, the bill passed both houses.

The liberal Duke of Gloucester, who spoke in favour of the bill, became the first President of the African Institution in July 1807. Evolving from the Sierra Leone Company, the Institution's charter stated its objectives as 'the civilization and improvement of Africa'[13] and 'the entire and universal Abolition of the Slave Trade'.[14] Its founding members included Zachary Macaulay, Lord Ellenborough, the bishops of London, Durham, Bath and Wells, the bankers Thomas Baring and R. Barclay, Henry Brougham, the younger William Pitt MP, Granville Sharp, Reverend Thomas Gisborne and the Nonconformist brewer Samuel Whitbread.[15]

The Institution aimed to 'prepare and fortify the minds of the ignorant natives of Africa against the fraudulent and mischievous efforts of eager and adventurous traffic',[16] and 'to promote the comforts of social life upon the sure basis of virtuous principle . . . as some compensation for the indescribable miseries which . . . Englishmen have inflicted upon the African race'.[17] Abroad, the Institution tried to persuade African traders to abandon slave trafficking for alternative commerce supplied by the businesses owned by its own members. To many African traders, it looked like the Europeans were trying to interfere with their private enterprise.[18] Back home, the Institution kept an eye out for abuses against abolition.[19]

On Thursday, 11 October, Zachary Macaulay wrote a letter to James Perry, the editor of the *Morning Chronicle*, the leading Whig daily newspaper. Born in 1768, the son of a Scottish priest, Macaulay devoted his life to the abolition of the 'abominable traffic',[20] awakened to the horrors of slavery by his youthful experiences on a sugar estate in Jamaica. He went to the island aged sixteen as a bookkeeper, was promoted to estate manager and then resigned in disgust. He once travelled as a passenger on an English slave ship bound for the West Indies, in order to witness for himself the horrors of the Middle Passage. His quarters were a hammock 'with a few slaves sleeping under it'.[21] To avoid the discovery of his damning record of the miserable journey, he kept his diary in Greek. In 1793, Macaulay became Governor of the new colony of liberated slaves, Sierra Leone, a position to which he was appointed by abolitionist leaders Wilberforce, Sharp and Henry Thornton, and which he held for six eventful years until returning to England in 1799.

Macaulay was one of the principal founders of London University, which he hoped would provide secular education for the sons of dissenters and those excluded by religion or other disqualification from the established universities. A fellow of the Royal Society, he counted Chateaubriand and Madame de Staël among his friends, and was an active member of all the leading Bible and missionary societies. Married to Selina Mills, Macaulay had nine children, including the Whig historian Thomas Babington Macaulay, who famously rejected his father's progressive stance on abolition and fair trade.[22]

Macaulay had been Secretary of the African Institution since its founding. From his study overlooking the leafy avenue of Clapham High Street, he penned the opening salvo in the battle to plead the cause of 'that wretched object advertised and publicly shewn [sic] for money – the Hottentot Venus'.[23] He had returned that afternoon from his first visit to 225 Piccadilly and was morally outraged.

Macaulay described witnessing a hateful tableau of degradation and exploitation between male master and black female slave, enacted at the heart of free London. Determined to prove that Saartjie was illegally transported and kept as a slave, Macaulay wanted to know 'under what circumstances she came to England and whether she was made a public spectacle with her own free will and consent, or whether she was compelled to exhibit herself and was desirous of returning to her own country'.[24] During his visit, Macaulay had questioned Cesars about Saartjie and asked how she came to be in England, performing in such a manner. She's a Hottentot, explained Cesars, obtained 'from the Dutch Boors' at the Cape, where 'he had made an agreement with the Government and they had given him permission to take her to this Country.' Macaulay declared himself 'much surprised' that she was brought to England with the consent of the Cape government. Are you sure, he pressed, that the Governor, Lord Caledon, gave his permission? Yes, he did, confirmed Cesars. Macaulay did not believe him and asked if Lord Caledon's permission was in writing; Cesars insisted that indeed it was.

Unconvinced, Macaulay, who was in regular correspondence with Lord Caledon, demanded that Cesars show him the signed permission, 'as he knew his hand writing'. Cesars expostulated: '. . . what, won't you believe my word? I have already told you that he has signed it and shall give you no further satisfaction . . . I do not choose to have so many questions put to me.' So saying, he left Macaulay to watch the remainder of the exhibition.[25]

Macaulay's letter ignited the press debate over Saartjie's status as free agent or slave:

> This poor female is made to walk, to *dance*, to shew herself, not for her own advantage, but for the profit of her master, when she appeared tired, holds up *a stick to her, like the wild beast keepers*, to intimidate her into obedience. I think, Sir, I have read some-where (but this you will know better than me), that the air of the British Constitution is too pure to permit slavery to exist where its influence extends. If that be the case, why is this poor creature to live under the most palpable and abject slavery in the very heart of the metropolis, for I am sure you will easily discriminate between those beings who are sufficiently degraded to show themselves for their *own* immediate profit, and where they act from their own free will; and this poor slave, who is obliged to shew herself, *to dance*, to be an object of the lowest ribaldry, by which her keeper is the only gainer. I am no advo-cate for these sights, on the contrary, I think it base in the extreme, that any human being should be thus exposed. It is contrary to every principle of morality or good order, but this exhibition connects the same offence to public decency, with that most horrid of all situations, *Slavery*.[26]

Saartjie had an important champion in Macaulay who was a leading member of the Clapham Sect. Active primarily

between 1790 and the 1830s, the Clapham Sect were evangelical Anglican Christians who campaigned for the
abolition of slavery, penal reform, moral regeneration, and
advanced missionary work both at home and abroad.
Deriving their name from the district in south-west London
where they were based, and known derisively as the
Clapham 'Saints', these wealthy businessmen and politicians
contributed in large part to the abolition of the slave trade
and slavery in Britain and its empire.

'Every friend to slavery knew Macaulay to be his most
dangerous foe,' wrote a fellow member of the Clapham Sect.
In Parliament, it was said, 'If the Negro should be eman-
cipated he would be more indebted to Mr Macaulay than
to any other man living.' And in 1833, on the passing of
the Emancipation Bill, Charles Buxton wrote to Macaulay,
'My sober and deliberate opinion is, that you have done
more towards this consummation than any other man.'[27]

Macaulay was editor of the Evangelical *Christian Observer*,
mouthpiece of the Clapham Sect, dedicated to supporting
the campaign against the slave trade, and, after 1807, the
exposure and destruction of the trade abroad. Championing
moral reform, the *Christian Observer* condemned theatre,
dancing and novel-reading. Macaulay was also an active
member of the Society for the Suppression of Vice, an
appropriate allegiance for the man to whom nothing was
funny. Founded in 1802 in order to avert the moral collapse
of the nation, this organisation was a direct successor to
the eighteenth-century anti-vice associations. It was quickly
denounced for only prosecuting the poor; one commentator
remarked that it should be renamed 'a society for
suppressing the vices of persons whose income does not

exceed £500 per annum'.[28] The Society waged war on 'profane swearers, Sabbath-breakers, and keepers of gambling resorts and brothels'. It proposed the suppression of lotteries, prosecution of those who were cruel to animals and those who used false weights and measures, the enforcement of Sabbath laws, and the suppression of 'the sale of objectionable books and prints'.[29]

Macaulay's active role in the society explains his objection that the exhibition of The Hottentot Venus twinned an 'offence to public decency' with the horrors of slavery. It was a formula resonant with Mary Wollstonecraft's argument, made fifteen years earlier in her *Vindication of the Rights of Women* (1792), that the sexual exploitation of women was akin to the condition of legal slavery. However, unlike Wollstonecraft, Macaulay was no supporter of women's rights.[30] In exhorting the friends of Liberty to defend Saartjie, Macaulay called for public censure of the wanton display of her spectacular flesh for entertainment in both person and print, as well as an investigation into her effectively enslaved status.

Prudery and prurience, though apparently antonyms, are common bedfellows. Wary of the feelings that her performance prompted in him, Macaulay was acutely aware of the sensual incitements of the Hottentot Venus exhibition. For all his self-conscious hauteur and unconscious paternalism, Macaulay was basically a decent man. The abolitionists understood that Saartjie, promoted as a quasi-scientific ethnographic curiosity, offered sexual tourism dressed up as education. Buffed, powdered, lubricated with glistening oil, trussed in her silk-and-cotton body stocking, adorned with feathers and beads, ethnically accessorised, face painted like a virgin sacrifice, Saartjie was got up as an embodied fetish, her trappings designed to accentuate her supposed 'idiosyncrasies and abnormalities'.[31] Through many Londoners' eyes she epitomised potent European fantasies about female African sexuality.

Macaulay asked his brother-in-law, the abolitionist priest Thomas Gisborne Babington, and the Cape-Dutch-speaking Peter van Wageninge to visit the exhibition and talk to Saartjie personally. Cesars confirmed that she could 'speak the Dutch language', but when van Wageninge attempted to question her directly, she refused to answer, presumably wary of talking in front of Cesars. She returned dejectedly to the stage and sighed deeply throughout her 'morose and sullen' performance. Babington and van Wageninge declared that she was clearly 'compleatly under restraint and controul and . . . deprived of her liberty'.[32]

Dunlop and Cesars hit back immediately at Macaulay's attack in the *Morning Chronicle* in a letter ghost-written by Dunlop and published under Cesars's name. 'I feel myself compelled, as a stranger,'[33] ventriloquised Dunlop, 'to refute this aspersion, for the vindication of my own character, and the satisfaction of the public.'[34] The letter argued of Macaulay:

In the first point, he betrays the greatest ignorance in regard to the Hottentot, who is as free as the English. This woman was my servant at the Cape, and not my slave, much less can she be so in England, where all breathe the air of freedom; she is brought here with her own free will and consent, to be exhibited for the joint benefit of both our families. That there may be no misapprehension on the part of the public, any person who can make himself understood to her is at perfect liberty to examine her, and know from herself whether she has not been always treated, not only with humanity, but the greatest kindness and tenderness.[35]

Dunlop was technically correct that Saartjie was Cesars's servant and not his slave. The Act for the Abolition of the Slave Trade of 25 March 1807 ruled explicitly on the matter of masters travelling with their slaves, stating that

the Act shall not extend to prevent any slave, who shall be really and truly the domestic servant of any person residing in any British island or colony, from attending his owner or master, or any part of his family, by sea, to any place whatever, whether under the dominion of his Majesty or of any foreign state.[36]

It further stipulated that 'domestic slaves serving on the person of any passengers on board'[37] were exempt from the requirement to have their names and occupations 'inserted in or indorsed upon the permit to depart'.[38] However, as a Khoisan, Saartjie was exempt from this exemption. As we have seen, Lord Caledon's 1809 proclamation established the status of protected servitude for Khoisan people and an official pass system regulating their movements. As a servant, Saartjie could have travelled without endorsement; as a Khoisan, she could not travel legitimately without Lord Caledon's personal authorisation.

Well aware of this, Macaulay demanded publicly that Cesars produce Saartjie's passport and, erroneously, dismissed as spurious his invitation to consult Saartjie directly on her situation 'because I do not think that there is in Europe a person who can make himself understood by the unfortunate object of the inquiry.'[39] Perhaps Macaulay thought Saartjie had not understood van Wageninge, rather than that she had refused to respond.

Macaulay insisted that Cesars 'state by what ship they were brought hither; and who, if any one, besides the Captain or person with whom he engaged for their passage, are acquainted with the circumstances of their coming on board'.[40] Here his instinct for skulduggery was correct. Macaulay knew from experience how frequently and easily ships' captains were bought off to assist in the transit of illegal passengers. Certain that Lord Caledon's office had never authorised Saartjie's departure, Macaulay allowed that she might have been enticed by wily persuasion, not physical force, to embark for England:

> If these circumstances be not satisfactorily cleared up, and if it should appear that a fellow-creature has been inveigled away from her home and country from motives disgraceful to human nature, all those who have been knowingly instrumental thereto, should be punished.[41]

Cesars continued to deny that he had brought Saartjie to England 'from her native country by force'.[42] He invited the public to visit 40 Haydn Square, the Minories, 'where they will have an opportunity of seeing my passport from Earl Caledon, Governor of the Cape of Good Hope; and they may be further satisfied on any other point respecting my conduct'.[43]

Determined to dissuade Africans from participating in the slave trade, the African Institution was particularly critical of

Cesars's role in Saartjie's exploitation. Macaulay knew that Cesars was of mixed ethnicity, as he made clear in a letter to the *Examiner* in which he compared Cesars with Shakespeare's Caliban. Despairing that the formerly oppressed might become a future oppressor, Macaulay attacked Cesars's greed: '. . . what, alas! will not avarice do? It is that "stamps the monster on the man," and leads him "to play such fantastic tricks as make the angels weep".'[44] Macaulay equally criticised Dunlop for betraying his medical calling. Rather than devoting himself to being 'a disinterested benefactor of his fellow-creatures', Dunlop had sold his soul for the love of gain, and made himself into a 'calculating, unfeeling speculator, eager to profit from their ignorance, vice or misfortune.'[45]

Saartjie's managers tried to resolve the scandal by removing Cesars from the scene. Once again impersonating Cesars, Dunlop wrote to the *Morning Chronicle* explaining that '. . . as my mode of proceeding at the place of public exhibition seems to have given offence to the Public, I have now given the sole direction of it to an Englishman, who now attends.'[46] However, this letter contradicted a statement made by William Bullock, who had recently collided with Dunlop in Piccadilly. At this encounter, Bullock had pointedly asked Dunlop about his involvement in the Hottentot Venus exhibition. Dunlop replied that he had 'been so unfortunate as to sell and dispose of his Interest in the exhibiting of the said Hottentot Woman and that he has now next to nothing to do with her'.[47] Dunlop resented the hypocrisy of rich merchant-capitalists with interests in African commerce dictating the morality of small-time entrepreneurs attempting their own forms of free commerce. 'Pray, Mr Editor,' he asked in the voice of Cesars, 'has she not as good a right to exhibit herself as an Irish Giant, or a Dwarf &c, &c?'[48]

Prompted by Bullock's information, Macaulay was determined to expose Dunlop. 'It is said,' he wrote to the press,

that she is, or rather was when abroad, the property of a Surgeon in the English navy, by whom her exhibitor Cezar [*sic*] is only employed. Sir, I do consider it necessary for the credit of our country that this affair be sifted to the end, and the real Agent be made to appear.[49]

The balladeers quickly picked up on Macaulay's campaign. Most popular was 'The storie of the Hottentot Ladie and her lawfull Knight, who essaied to release her out of captivitie, and what my lordes the judges did therein', which cast Macaulay in the role of the chivalrous Sir Vikar, 'lawfull Knight',[50] intent on releasing his 'Hottentot Ladie' from captivity. It began by announcing a lady of renown, 'THE VENUS HOTTENTOT', a great rarity living in 'Piccadillie', and explained that her 'rump', 'large as a cauldron pot . . . is why men go to see, this lovely HOTTENTOT':

> Now this was shewn for many a day,
> And eke for many a night;
> Till sober folks began to say,
> That all could not be right.
> Some said, this was with her good will;
> Some said, that it was not;
> And asked why did they use so ill
> This ladie HOTTENTOT.

At last a doughty Knight stood forth,
Sir Vikar was his name;
A knight of singular good worth,
Of faire and courtly fame.
With him the laws of chivalrie
Were not so much forgot;
But he would try most gallantly,
To serve the HOTTENTOT.[51]

The offstage dramas at the Hottentot Venus exhibition had become as diverting as the main attraction. Fought over like a disputed territory, Saartjie had no voice in the press debate over her freedom. By going to law, the African Institution aimed to give her an opportunity to have her say. Saartjie, an immigrant from a British colony and a member of a subject people, was about to become the first black South African woman whose right to liberty would be put to the test of the constitutional rule of law in Britain. She was about to find herself at the centre of the most contentious court case about illegal slavery since abolition.

7

THE CASE OF THE HOTTENTOT VENUS

On Wednesday, 17 October 1810, Zachary Macaulay, Thomas Gisborne Babington and Peter van Wageninge visited the barrister Sir Simon Le Blanc[1] at his chambers in Serjeant's Inn, Chancery Lane, London, to file an affidavit in support of their application for a writ of habeas corpus[2] to be issued on Saartjie's 'keepers'. They demanded that Cesars be made to provide proof of Saartjie's passport from Lord Caledon, the name of the ship on which she had travelled, and an indication as to 'whether any individuals at the "Cape," or elsewhere, are acquainted with the circumstances of their embarkation'.[3] Satisfied that Cesars's evasions revealed his guilt, Macaulay publicised the intention of the African Institution to utilise one of the fundamental tenets of the British rule of law safeguarding the liberty of the subject: 'I am persuaded no English Judge would refuse a Habeas Corpus, which should assert the right of humanity.'[4]

Saartjie's abolitionist champions were determined to prove that she was compelled to exhibit herself without her free will and consent. They also wanted to know if she was 'desirous of returning to her own country as the said Institution would be anxious in that case to restore her to her Country and friends'.[5] The *Examiner* asked: 'Might not the Missionary Society do much by having this woman, who is very young, instructed, and then sent back to her native land?'[6] Saartjie, no doubt, would have had her own views on being sent to Bible school in Clapham.

Macaulay's affidavit emphasised his disapproval of Saartjie's apparel: 'Her dress is so tight, that her shapes above and the enormous size of her posterior parts are as visible as if the said female were naked, and the dress is evidently intended to give her the appearance of her being undressed.' He then focussed on the subject of Saartjie's bottom. Her 'Exhibitor', he explained,

> would invite the spectators to feel her posterior parts and . . . would desire her to turn round in order that every body might see her extraordinary shape . . . [S]he is exhibited to the public in the same manner that any animal of the brute creation would be exhibited.[7]

Babington and van Wageninge provided the additional details that the audience 'are invited to feel her posterior parts to satisfy themselves that no art is practiced'.[8]

The abolitionists refuted Cesars's defence that Saartjie was his servant, not his slave, and therefore 'as free as the English'.[9] Macaulay published an essay in the *Examiner* arguing that the condition of slavery was a matter of kind, not degree. For a member of a subject race to be treated like a slave, he proposed, was in effect the same as actually being a legal slave. The argument that their human chattels were 'happier' in subjection was the old cant of slave owners:

> [I]s the capture and exhibition of this Hottentot many degrees removed from the barbarous and illegal practices of the Slave Trade? She is said by her keeper, in a vindicatory letter, to be happy even in her present degrading situation: this reminds me of the rat catcher, who, when accused of cruelty in sewing up the chops of his weasel, replied, oh master, he is so used to it that he loves it, expects it, and would be uncomfortable without it. Indeed this argument is too stale and thread-worn to be accepted now. It was the old rallying point of those who vindicated that abomination of our land the Slave Trade: The slaves are not so miserable as you think them to be: come and see them happy under our *kind and generous protection* . . . Let the honour of Englishmen rescue their character from the disgrace of keeping a foreigner, and a female too, in worse than Egyptian bondage.[10]

The African Institution intended to use Saartjie's case as a means to draw attention to the escalating infringements of the Abolition Acts that went unpunished, undermining Britain's moral and political status as abolitionist pioneer. Stories about illegal slave ships, easily bribed captains and human contraband were common,[11] and by 1810 lacked sufficient novelty to keep the question of illegal trade in the headlines. The Hottentot Venus, however, was a story of illegal transportation involving an iconic personality.

William Bullock's testimony was crucial, providing the evidence of Dunlop's intention to sell Saartjie as a commodity that the Institution needed to prove her slave status. Bullock knew Macaulay, and both, as we have seen, knew Banks. Macaulay wrote to the *Examiner*, '[I]f it can be proved that the Hottentot has been offered to sale, this of itself would alone burst her fetters.'[12]

The Banks connection proved significant. In 1803, continuing his interest in the indigenous people of the Cape Colony, Banks held a reception at his mansion for the Khoisan missionaries Mary and John Cornelius van Rooyen and Martha Arendse, who were visiting London. These well-known converts from the Zak River area of the eastern Cape[13] travelled to England 'to converse personally with the [London Missionary] Society and others of the Lord's people on the subject of Salvation'.[14] The diarist Joseph Farington, invited to meet them, seemed a little disappointed that the 'Hottentot' visitors were not more exotic. The Van Rooyens and Arendse, he recalled, engaged mostly in a polite, dull conversation with Lady Banks and Miss Banks, mediated by the Dutch missionary Kircherer, who was hosting their visit. 'They were dressed,' Farington said, 'in the English manner,' and 'their manner was as decent and as well regulated as well ordered Country people of our own could be.'[15] These starched missionaries had testified and held public debates at St James's Church, a few steps away from where Saartjie was living and performing. Like these respectable Khoisan missionaries known by Banks and his circle, Saartjie was also from the eastern Cape. Unlike them, she was an apparently godless showgirl.

The case of The Hottentot Venus opened at the Court of the King's Bench[16] in Westminster Hall on 24 November 1810.[17] Silk gowns, horsehair wigs and brushed whiskers assembled with a rustling, bristling air of impatience; this was a Saturday sitting. Lanterns and some supplementary candles gave dim resistance to the dull winter day. Stirred by news of the hearings, a large queue formed outside 225 Piccadilly, where Saartjie performed as usual.

Sir Simon Le Blanc represented the African Institution. The aptly named Edward Law, the first Baron Ellenborough, Lord Chief Justice of England (appointed in 1802) and founder-member of the African Institution, presided as judge.[18] Notably, Lord Ellenborough had earlier in the year presided over William Cobbett's famous seditious libel trial.[19]

Attorney General Sir William Garrow rose to make an application on behalf of 'this unfortunate female, who was exhibited to the public under circumstances of peculiar disgrace to a civilized country.'[20] His clients believed that the Hottentot Venus exhibition violated public decorum and insulted human nature. The court, he urged, would learn that the unfortunate female was brought unwillingly from her own country, kept in England for exhibition without her consent, and appeared compliant only as a result of the menaces and ill treatment to which she was constantly subjected. His clients wanted to liberate Saartjie from her confinement, place her under proper protection while she remained in England and restore her to her country 'by the first conveyance offered'. No one could doubt that The Hottentot Venus was kept in a state of confinement, and his clients wished Saartjie to know that she was not destitute of friends and had the support of men who were the friends of all humanity.[21]

Brandishing the affidavits of Bullock, Macaulay,

Babington and van Wageninge, Garrow said that a writ of habeas corpus should be issued on Saartjie's captors. Given the circumstances, however, he suggested that bringing The Hottentot Venus before the court might offend both her sensibilities and the former's delicacy. Her keepers, Garrow continued, must demonstrate why they should not be subject to the 'Great Writ' and must agree to allow her to be interviewed by 'persons who understood her language' without them being present.

In applying for a writ of habeas corpus, the African Institution was following established precedent in cases involving the legality of slavery in England. Slaves had been bought and displayed at the Elizabethan and Stuart courts, advertised for sale through most of the eighteenth century and would be bequeathed in wills as late as the 1820s. However, Lord Chief Justice Holt in the early eighteenth century had opined that 'as soon as a Negro comes into England, he becomes free,'[22] and in 1762 the Lord Chancellor had stated that 'as soon as a man puts foot on English ground, he is free: a negro may maintain an action against his master for ill usage, and may have a Habeas Corpus, if restrained of his liberty.'[23]

Although habeas corpus had been used in previous cases concerning illegal slavery, it was Lord Mansfield's judgement in the case of James Somerset in 1772 that consolidated its use. Led by Granville Sharp, this test case between the West India merchants and the abolitionists determined conclusively that slavery could not exist in England. Somerset, a slave brought from Virginia to England by his owner, escaped but was then recaptured, bound in irons and due to be shipped to Jamaica. The Court of the King's Bench issued a writ of habeas corpus on the ship's captain, requiring him to present Somerset to the court. Somerset's counsel, Serjeant-at-Law William Davys at the Court of King's Bench, claimed that 'England was too pure an Air for a Slave to breathe in.'[24] Macaulay's stirring rhetoric about the right of The Hottentot Venus to breathe free air over England was a direct reference to the Somerset case.[25]

Winning Saartjie's trust was essential. As Garrow argued, she might be justifiably suspicious and hostile to being made to appear, yet again, as a spectacle, this time in the unfamiliar and intimidating environment of a grand courtroom. Equally, the African Institution seemed afraid that the infamous Venus, denied decent clothes by her exploiters, could not be relied upon to appear in court appropriately dressed. After all, as the affidavits attested, her performance costume was indecent. At this, Lord Ellenborough raised his bushy eyebrows.

'She is so tightly habited?' he asked with interest.

'Yes, My Lord, so as absolutely to appear as if she were naked,' replied Garrow. 'She is dressed in a colour as nearly resembling her skin as possible. The dress is contrived to exhibit the entire frame of her body, and the spectators are even desired to touch particular parts of her person.'

Lord Ellenborough scanned the affidavits. 'And does it state that she shews a feeling of pain from that circumstance? I do not call for what might be an indelicate exposure; but only desire to know if the mode of exhibition be such as to give pain to a sensitive mind.' The court agreed that Saartjie's state of mind could only be discovered by interviewing her directly. On the question of whether the show was an offence to public decency, Le Blanc reminded the court, the defendants could only be made to answer this under a separate criminal charge.

Lord Ellenborough considered the question of Saartjie providing her own statement. 'Is it ascertained that she speaks Dutch?' he asked Garrow, who confirmed that Cesars had stated that Saartjie understood 'Low Dutch' (i.e. Afrikaans). Lord Ellenborough pursued the question: 'Have you nobody who speaks what may be termed her own vernacular tongue?' It may not be easy to find such a native speaker, he suggested, but it was necessary, as the language in which the keeper had been heard to address Saartjie may merely have been words of command, 'a language which it is well known is easily taught'. However, Macaulay made a mistake in his evidence when he asserted his suspicion 'that Hendrik Cesars himself can only make her comprehend him by threats and signs'. Macaulay did not realise that the Afrikaans (known also as Low or 'kitchen' Dutch) in which Saartjie and Hendrik conversed fluently was in fact the indigenous language of slaves, servants, free blacks and urban workers at the Cape. Macaulay was also mistaken when he said that he did 'not think that there is in Europe a person who can make himself understood by the unfortunate object of the inquiry'. As it turned out, there were in fact Afrikaans-speakers in cosmopolitan London able to translate.[26]

Macaulay was concerned that the court might be misled by the deceptive 'softness' of Saartjie's hands, and worried that 'her being able to dance and to play on some sort of musical instrument, do not exactly coincide with the idea of her being a slave.' Lord Ellenborough insisted that the court must ascertain directly from Saartjie herself whether or not she experienced 'pain at the exposure to which she is

subjected'. The court then asked what would happen to her
should it be established that she was in fact being detained
in a state of slavery. When brought up under habeas corpus,
Saartjie could go where she pleased – 'and where,' asked Le
Blanc, 'is she to go?' Garrow confirmed that there were
persons 'ready to take her, and she is to be told so'. He moved
that Saartjie be brought before the court 'in order to declare
from her own mouth whether her present situation is voluntary or compelled'. Le Blanc supported her right to
self-determination: 'She is to be left to judge for herself.'

Delaring that the court must come to know Saartjie's
mind and was interested only in her true situation, Lord
Ellenborough granted the rule:

[I]t is ordered, that Tuesday next be given to Alexander
Dunlop and Hendrik Cesar [*sic*], to shew cause why a writ of
habeas corpus should not issue directed to them, commanding
them to have the body of a certain native of South Africa,
denominated the Hottentot Venus, before the court immediately, to undergo, &c . . . And it is further ordered, that one
or two such person or persons as shall be approved for that
purpose by the coroner and attorney, have free access to the
said native of South Africa at the house of the said Alexander
Dunlop and Hendrik Cesar in York Street Piccadilly, in the
absence of the said Alexander Dunlop and Hendrick Cesar, but
in the presence of one or two such persons as shall be nomi-
nated by them, and to be approved of by the said coroner and
attorney for the purpose of conversing with her.

The case adjourned for the weekend.

*   *   *

Using the profits from the Hottentot Venus show, Dunlop and Cesars hired the services of junior barrister Stephen Gaselee for their defence. Gaselee instructed them to make sure that Saartjie had a proper business contract and to ensure that the court could be persuaded that Cesars had been removed from the exhibition.

Tuesday, 27 November 1810, was a momentous day for Saartjie.

Dunlop took her to Sweeting's Alley at the Royal Exchange to see Arend Jacob Guitard, a Dutch-speaking public notary. Dunlop presented Guitard with an agreement drawn up between Saartjie and himself, dated 29 October, and asked him to translate it into Dutch and then read it out to her to confirm that it was to her satisfaction. Crucially, the contract began with the stipulation that it was backdated to 20 March 1810, the same day that Dunlop received permission from the Governor's office, approved by Lord Caledon, to depart from the Cape 'together with his servant'.[27] Under her contract, 'Saartjie Baartman', in addition to 'performing such domestic duties as her master might reasonably demand of her',[28] agreed to allow herself 'to be viewed by the public of Ireland and England "just as she was"'. Dunlop committed to pay all the expenses of the voyage and to give Saartjie, in case of illness, 'all the care and all such medicines as she might require', as well as 'to defray the cost of repatriating her should she desire to return to her own country'. Significantly, the terms of the contract covered Saartjie's key concerns during that autumn of 1810; profit-sharing, her need for warmer clothes, better medical treatment and the guarantee that she would be sent home. Guitard read

Saartjie his translation 'twice plainly and distinctly' and claimed to be satisfied that she understood the contents. He then interviewed her, detailing the conversation in an affidavit. Was she contented with her situation, and did she have enough good food and drink? Yes, she replied to all his questions.

> And this deponent also asked the said Saartjie Baartman whether she preferred either to return to the Cape of Good Hope or stay in England, and [to] that she replied – Stay here.[29]

That same afternoon, five well-heeled, well-fed eminences presented themselves at Saartjie's York Street lodgings. Dunlop and Cesars were forbidden to attend. Afrikaans-speaking Samuel Solly and John George Moojen, both merchants, were translators for, respectively, the African Institution and Dunlop and Cesars. James Templer, Coroner of the Court of the King's Bench, supervised the proceedings. Gaselee and Le Blanc represented their clients. The inquisitory procedure undertaken to interview Saartjie was required to be thorough and scrupulous. The penalties for trifling with legal procedures were horrendous, so everyone had to take care to relay truthfully what they observed and recorded.

Saartjie was interviewed in 'Low' Dutch (Afrikaans), which, Solly and Moojen confirmed, 'she perfectly understood.' The conversation lasted for three hours. (The fact that Saartjie doubled as maidservant at York Street begs the question of who served the tea at this lengthy interview.) This occasion inspired press myths that cast Saartjie into the role of destiny's controlling heroine. She appeared, it was rumoured, 'magnificently attired',[30] offered her guests presents, and forcefully declared that she had came to, and remained in, England by her own free will.[31]

Saartjie recounted her childhood and early life at the Cape. She came to England, she asserted, 'by her own consent . . . and was promised half of the money for exhibiting her person' for a period of six years, and, she claimed, 'went personally to the government in company with Hendrik Cesars to ask permission to go to England'. So saying, Saartjie presented her new contract with Dunlop to the assembled auditors. Mr Dunlop, she explained directly to Solly and Moojen, had promised to pay for her to go home in six years' time, 'the money belonging to her with her'. In the meantime, she was 'kindly treated' and, apart from the fact that she needed warmer clothes, had no complaints. She had 'no desire whatever of returning to her own country' and would rather stay in England 'because she likes the country and has money given her by her master.' She claimed that no violence or threats had been used against her, and stressed that she was treated modestly and enjoyed her Sunday coach rides. But Solly and Moojen were unconvinced:

> To the various questions we put to her whether if she chose at any time to discontinue her person being exhibited, she might do so, we could not draw a satisfactory answer from her. She understands very little of the agreement made with her by Mr Dunlop on the 29th October and which agreement she produced to us.

They were at pains to enter a specific concluding clause to the transcript of Saartjie's interview, stressing that she had informed them that 'she could neither read nor write.'

The court reconvened on Wednesday, 29 October. Gaselee opened on behalf of Dunlop and Cesars. He would show that Saartjie Baartman (referred to by her own name for the first time in court) was neither kept under improper restraint nor a slave brought unwillingly or illegally from the Cape. If, after he had presented the evidence, the court should still think that she was treated with 'anything like cruelty', his clients 'were willing to give her up at once'.

Gaselee, on whom Dickens based the irascible Justice Stareleigh of Bordell v Pickwick, was 'a skilful special pleader' who later became a judge (1824), received a knighthood (1825) and was Vice-president of the Royal Humane Society. So short and so fat 'that he seemed all face and waistcoat,'[32] he had small eyes, a broad pink face and a bobbing head. About her height, he must have looked both menacing and comical to Saartjie as he inspected her with his 'queer little eyes'.[33]

Gaselee laid out the essence of his clients' defence. Since the African Institution had lodged its affidavit on 17 October, Mr Alexander Dunlop had taken over the direction of Saartjie's exhibition from Mr Hendrik Cesars, due to the incident in which Cesars had allegedly intimidated Saartjie by raising his hand to her. Following this complaint, Cesars had 'been removed from his situation' as master of ceremonies and with him, Gaselee implied, the threat of physical violence against her.

Gaselee addressed the court on the subject of slavery and the freedom of human beings in England. To emphasise her identity as a free subject, he called Saartjie by her proper name. Saartjie was not, as slaves had been in the eighteenth century, an object of displayed merchandise exploitable for the profit of others but a free woman who displayed herself willingly on condition that she receive a share of the profits from her exhibition. Gaselee could confirm from her own affidavit that she was promised her portion. So anxious were his clients to prove that Saartjie was not held under constraint that they welcomed the interference of the court and would do anything to satisfy its demands.

In this spirit, his clients invited the Institution to independently appoint a trustee to manage Saartjie's income and disburse her allowance and annuity as they saw fit. This suggestion revealed the prejudicial assumption that Saartjie was incapable of managing her income. She was a woman, she was black, and she was a 'Hottentot'. Saartjie's right, and understanding of how, to make money was one thing, her questionable ability to manage it apparently quite another. The Institution declined the offer, as Gaselee suspected they would. Committed to defending public morality, they could not undertake to administer what they regarded as immoral earnings from entertainment that was, in their eyes, virtually prostitution.

Gaselee moved to the question of whether the Hottentot Venus exhibition was *contra bonos mores* (against good morals). Saartjie stated in her affidavit that there was nothing indecent about her appearance. The complaint that her 'thin silk dress' was too revealing was inaccurate. It covered her body, and underneath it she wore 'a covering of cotton'. However, Saartjie had requested warmer clothes, and this demand would be met.

Gaselee presented to the Attorney General the results of the interview with Saartjie, Dunlop's affidavit and Saartjie's contract. This evidence brought the case to a legal but not a moral resolution. Garrow conceded that Dunlop and Cesars had met the requirements of the court. Saartjie was 'plainly not under restraint', and as she had apparently given her consent to be exhibited, the court could interfere no further. Moreover, he added in telling reference to Saartjie's assumed delinquency, if she were set at liberty, 'the only effect of taking her from her keepers would be to let her loose to go back again.'

The case turned on the question of whether Saartjie had the right to sell herself, and whether, as a subordinated subject, she was capable of giving her consent to do so. In slavery, 'the buyer gives nothing, the seller receives nothing.'[34] Saartjie had apparently agreed to a contract that guaranteed her an annual wage. From Elizabethan times, English legal precedent held that a person might enter into a contract of service for life but not sell himself as a slave, as the rules governing servitude by contract would 'not permit the servant to incorporate into his contract the ingredients of slavery'.[35] These judgements were intended to protect the liberty of individuals who wished to sell their labour in perpetuity whilst preventing any possibility that a person might legitimately consent to become a slave. The distinction was crucial to the ideology of free-market capitalism. A person could sell his labour, though not himself, even if in receipt of his wages he remained perpetually dependent.

Rousseau would scoff. Consent was a myth disguising the fraud and coercion by which most of humankind was subordinated. No one except a lunatic would consent to their own bondage.[36] But, as Garrow said, the application for the writ of habeas corpus could not be sustained now that Saartjie's sworn affidavit of contract and consent had been presented. The court therefore agreed that she could voluntarily degrade herself for the price agreed; the law would interfere no further. Because she gave her labour willingly, she was deemed free although clearly dependent.

The issues of contract and consent in Saartjie's case were complicated by the fact that she was protected by Lord Caledon's 1809 proclamation on the registration and contracting into service of 'Hottentots' in the Cape colony.[37] Garrow pointed out that Cesars had registered Saartjie as a servant before a magistrate as the law required, but while 'a free servant might leave the Cape . . . no Hottentot would be permitted to do so.' Cesars had not applied for permission for her to leave. Lord Caledon had been furious when he discovered Saartjie's illegal departure and for what purpose she had been taken to England. 'The matter,' Lord Ellenborough pronounced disapprovingly, 'was allowed by an interior person in office there.' That 'interior person' was the duped and scapegoated Henry Alexander, the Governor's secretary.

Summing up his judgement, Lord Ellenborough cautioned Dunlop and Cesars to treat Saartjie well, or, he threatened – referring to the widely publicised incident of Cesars's bullying – 'the law would direct its arm with uplifted resentment against the offending parties.' Supposed to be under restraint, Saartjie had 'in express terms declared the reverse'. It seemed to the court that she had no desire to change her situation or return home immediately. Therefore, Dunlop and Cesars must pay her as contracted, and for 'as long as she consented to the exhibition'.

In closing, Lord Ellenborough offered the African Institution a recommendation for further action: 'If there be any offence to decency in the exhibition that comes in another way: – that may be the ground of a prosecution.' This was an invitation to the Clapham Sect to bring a charge of public indecency against Saartjie's exhibition. But they never did. To institute a private prosecution on grounds of indecency would have been difficult, costly and risky.[38]

The Clapham Sect romanticised Saartjie as a dispossessed child of Africa, yearning for her heritage, fallen from a graceful state of atavistic noble savagery to crude sexual, scientific exploitation in the modern factory of sin that was central London. In their eyes, she had no benefits from exile but was entirely degraded by her display. At the outset of the trial, they had sentimentalised her as a victim of Cesars's and Dunlop's concupiscence: now they judged her a victim of her own concupiscence. Saartjie's response to the case brought on her behalf suggests a combination of naive obstinacy with sanguine practicality. The white wigs might argue over whether she was slave or freewoman, but Saartjie knew that she was seller and commodity in one, and must take care of herself.[39]

The abolitionists lost their case. Saartjie won herself a contract, written security of profit-sharing, warmer clothes and passage home. Business at 225 Piccadilly continued as usual.

Publicity generated by the case ensured the Hottentot Venus show's success for the duration of the winter. The press suggested that SAARTJEE had bested both the free-marketeers who exploited her and the abolitionists who sought to send her to Bible school. Saartjie now symbolised the belief that the former slave-turned-wage labourer was a free individual. Her 'bright gold' and suggestively pendulous money-bags featured as motifs in many popular cartoons that covered the outcome of the trial. For the first time, Saartjie was depicted in fashionable European dress, an heiress besieged by fortune-hunters. She was seen not as a sympathetic victim but as a dextrous businesswoman who had outmanoeuvred her managers and made herself attractive to eligible bachelors as a woman of style and means.

In historical terms, the conclusion of Saartjie's case was a compromise in favour of free-market capitalism. Had she brokered the best result possible for herself, given the choices, or was she now doubly enslaved? When Saartjie said to Solly and Moojen that she wanted to stay in England, was she speaking against her true wishes, as a prisoner under duress, and for fear of reprisal from Dunlop and Cesars? Experience had taught her to keep her expectations low and to trust no one. She understood that the men who had taken her managers to court offered release from exhibiting herself and would send her home. Yet she regarded the offer with suspicion. What did they want in return? Macaulay and the abolitionists assumed Saartjie's desire to return to South Africa before they had ever asked her what *she* wanted. The outcome of the case suggests that she demanded the rights of the working immigrant to be paid for her labour and enjoy, if only temporarily, the comparative benefits of exile.

Caricature engraving by Charles Williams from 1811, published in 1822, satirising the notion of an association between a Hottentot Venus and *eros*. With its plump white baby Cupid carried by Saartjie, the image inadvertently alludes to Saartjie's past as a domestic servant and nursemaid in a racially divided colonial society.

A crowded street in London, by George Cruikshank, 1812, shows the bustling intensity of London life and its popular entertainments. Note the shopfront poster advertising 'The Hottentot Venus' show.

Coloured aquatint by Frederick Christian Lewis,
published in March 1811, shortly before The Hottentot
Venus went on tour. Saartjie is shown wearing the
numerous accessories transported from South Africa by
Dunlop and Cesars in which she was to be exhibited.

Political cartoon by Charles Williams depicting Saartjie and Lord Grenville going into business together shortly after her court case, London, December 1810. Grenville and his Whig cohorts had been known as the broad bottoms since the 1806 'Ministry of all the Talents', hence the proliferation of cartoons featuring both him and Saartjie.

Satirical engraving of Miss Ridsdale, 'Sartjee' and Miss Harvey by William Heath, 1810, parodying three famous London courtesans – Henriette Dubochet, her sister Fanny and her friend Julia Johnstone – who were known at the time as 'The Three Graces'. Speculations on Saartjie's impressions of London became a popular subject for satire, offering an opportunity to poke fun at native English culture.

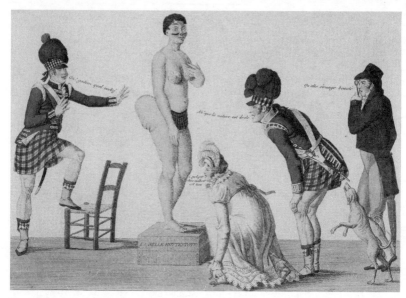

Unattributed cartoon, Paris, 1814, showing what Parisians regarded as another 'curiosity': Scots Guards, serving in the allied army of occupation. French audiences both feared and admired Saartjie's distinctive difference, making her an instant success.

Saartjie's state funeral, Hankey, Eastern Cape, 9 August 2002.

As an alternative to living under British colonial rule in the Cape, there were advantages to being in London. In the Cape colony, Saartjie was enserfed by the special care of the Governor and classed as 'imbecilic' Hottentot. In London, she was no longer a subjugated Khoisan servant, but promised wages beyond her expectations, and had now become one of the city's most recognisable figures. It is sensible to assume that she hoped and dreamed of returning home. Most exiles do. But what in reality did she have to go back to in Cape Town, apart from the certainty of continued drudgery under white colonial rule, stirring the pot and raking ashes from the inferno of domestic servitude?

'Neptune's Last Resource', cartoon by Charles Williams, December 1811, depicting the Duke of Clarence proposing to Saartjie. A notorious fortune-hunter, the duke had famously been turned down by at least nine heiresses, and at the time of the cartoon was averaging about one unsuccessful marriage proposal per month.

8

CACHE-SEXE

On Tuesday, 30 April 1811, the following announcement appeared in the London *Morning Post*:

THE HOTTENTOT VENUS takes her FINAL DEPAR-TURE in a FEW WEEKS from this Metropolis, which accounts for the crowds of Fashionables, particularly of her own sex, who daily attend the Exhibition, the false idea of indelicacy being now entirely, and very properly, got over, from her having been visited as a truly interesting object of natural curiosity by some of the first Ladies of Distinction in the Kingdom. Her contour and formation certainly surpass any thing of the kind ever seen in Europe, or perhaps ever produced on the face of the earth. [Those] who have not seen this most wonderful uncommon creature, will lament their want of curiosity after her departure.[1]

Saartjie's court case boosted the show's popularity. In November 1810, a Christmas pantomime entitled *The Hottentot Venus: or Harlequin in Africa* had opened to appreciative audiences in London, afterwards touring the provinces.[2] Saartjie's appearance in a deck of playing cards, singing and dancing before a beaming, appreciative male audience whose fifty-two subjects were chosen to typify London life in 1811 attests to the fact that she 'had danced her way into the mainstream of popular culture in the metropolis'.[3]

A dramatic change in Dunlop's professional circumstances made his threesome with Saartjie and Cesars entirely dependent on her labour. Embarrassed by Dunlop's public exposure of Lord Caledon's maladministration which allowed Saartjie to depart South Africa illegally, the surjeon's military employers axed him; on 25 December 1810 he was placed on half-pay, with no prospect of a new posting. The powerful closed ranks around Lord Caledon, protected him from personal investigation and punished Dunlop by finally destroying his already precarious military career.

Summer was approaching – the traditional touring season for entertainers, freaks and wonders. Fairs, pleasure gardens and outdoor amusements promised fresh audiences and lower overheads. The exhibition at 225 Piccadilly closed in May 1811, and for the next three years, until the summer of 1814, The Hottentot Venus toured Britain. In 'The Humours of Bartlemy Fair', Saartjie is described as one of the key attractions: 'Here, here, the only booth in the fair, for the greatest curiosity in all the known world – the Vonderful and surprising Hottentot Wenus is here, who measures three yards and three quarters round.'[4] A Cruikshank cartoon shows Saartjie on the playbill of summer entertainments for the royal court at the Pavillion in Brighton.[5] 'The Address of Jack Higginbottom in behalf of himself and the Hottent Venus, to the Ladies of Bath', which poked merciless fun at the Clapham Saints, places Saartjie in Bath during the same summer. On 28 August 1811 the Reverend Halloran made a reference in his diary to Saartjie's touring around the country, managed by Dunlop.[6] Then, at the end of the year, she unexpectedly appeared in a cathedral.

On the cold morning of 1 December 1811, before a crammed Sunday congregation and under the lofty Gothic arches of the Collegiate and Parish Church of Christ in Manchester, Saartjie was baptised. The chaplain who christened her was none other than the eccentric divine Reverend Joshua Brookes. Brookes was almost as short as Saartjie, and the cathedral's ancient and imposing stone font was taller than them both. For twenty-two years Saartjie had been Saartjie Baartman from the Gamtoos River. On this Sunday, better heeled than any other black working-class Mancunian, she entered the Christian church and was given an Anglicised forename: Sarah.

One of Anglican England's best-known priests, Brookes was a contumacious, gleeful eccentric, widely respected and many times memorialised in fiction. Short, dark and stumpy with bushy, grown-together eyebrows, he was nicknamed 'Knave of Clubs' and spoke in a broad Mancunian dialect, except from the pulpit. Mrs Linnaeus Banks memorably described him as 'a rough, crusted, unpolished, black-diamond, hasty in temper, harsh in tone, blunt in speech and in the pulpit, but with a true heart beating under the angular external crystals'.[7] He munched on sweets and fresh pastries while conducting funeral services, violently punched the ears

December 1. Sarah Bartmann a Female Hottentot from the Colony of the Cape of Good Hope, born on the Borders of Caffraria, baptized this Day by Permission of the Lord Bishop of Chester in a Letter from his Lordship to Jos. Brookes Chaplain.

This is to certify that the above is a true Copy, extracted from the Register of the Collegiate and Parish-Church of Christ, in Manchester, this seventh Day of December 1811

Witness Joshua Brookes

Chaplain of the Collegiate and Parish-church of Christ, in Manchester.

ASTON, PRINTER, MANCHESTER.

Sarah Bartmann est morte à Paris le 5 Janvier 1816 son corps a été donné par Monsieur Réaux au Museum d'histoire naturelle ou l'on a conservé son squelette et son corps moulé.

Saartjie's baptismal certificate, Manchester, December 1811, which was found among her effects when she died in Paris on Friday 29 December 1815 (note how it has been folded small for carrying).

of his schoolboy pupils, was a noted bibliophile, and collected 'tasteless', 'tawdry' and indecent engravings.[8] Yet for all his studied eccentricity, he worked hard, and 'married, christened, and buried more people during his ministry than all the other ecclesiastics put together'.[9]

The cathedral's baptismal register for 1811 contains a uniquely detailed annotation:

Sarah Bartmann, a Female Hottentot from the Colony of the Cape of Good Hope, born on the Borders of Caffraria, baptized this Day by Permission of the Lord Bishop of Chester in a Letter from his Lordship to Jos. Brookes Chaplain.[10]

Because special permission was required from the bishopric to baptise a person who was not a local parishioner, Brookes wrote to the Bishop of Chester, Bowyer Edward Sparke, laying out the special situation. Sadly, their correspondence was destroyed when the cathedral was bombed during the Blitz. Sparke had a suggestive but inconclusive connection to South Africa. His nephew, William Jones, served in the first British occupation of the Cape colony. In 1796, as we have seen, Jones had written a detailed letter to his eminent uncle in England, remarking on everything from the state of the garrison at Saldhana Bay to the ribbons and frills of the society ladies of Cape Town. This epistle also contained his view of 'Hottentot women'.

The intrigued press reported Saartjie's christening and speculated as to 'who were the sponsors of this extraordinary occasion'.[11] The following Saturday, Saartjie collected the official baptismal certificate, signed by her sponsor, Dunlop. She remained visible in the press, politics and popular culture, but the real Saartjie disappeared almost entirely from public view, suggesting that her baptism was precipitated by an important development in her personal life, of which there is no record. Perhaps she was pregnant, planning to get married or both. It is unclear, though, why a press so eager to remark on her baptism would not have leapt on the opportunity to report her wedding, particularly given their perennial obsession with her eligibility as an heiress.

In April 1812 Saartjie appeared in Ireland, performing for five days in the city of Limerick, where, 'much to the credit of the people', she 'was visited by very few'.[12] That she was on show four months after her baptism does not rule out the possibility that she was pregnant and subsequently gave birth to a second child. If she did, it never became public knowledge. There has been speculation that Saartjie and Dunlop married, but no evidence to support this supposition has been found.

Saartjie re-emerged in Portsmouth in the summer of 1812, at Dunlop's bedside. On 18 July, he died of unknown causes,[13] freeing Saartjie and Cesars from their dependency on him. Dunlop's military pension ceased on his death, and he appears to have had no remaining contact with his family. It seems that he left whatever money and effects he had to Cesars and Saartjie. Lord Ellenborough had made Dunlop guarantor of Saartjie's contract. With his death, she lost her only legal surety that she would get home.

From July 1812, Saartjie disappeared without trace. These were her last years of anonymity. In 1814 she reappeared, in a blaze of publicity; thenceforward she would remain permanently in the public gaze for two centuries.

* * *

In the first week of January 1816, Napoleon's luxurious bullet-proof carriage, 'dark blue and gilt, with vermillion wheels',[14] went on display at the Egyptian Hall in Piccadilly, complete with the coachman who had lost an arm in its capture by a Prussian ambush, two concussed horses, the Emperor's folding camp-bed, and sundry personal possessions, including diamonds, leather bottles, gold pieces and an unused 'cake of Windsor soap'.[15]

The carriage was a gift from the Prussians to the cash-strapped Prince Regent, who promptly sold it to William Bullock for £2,500. Bullock in turn put it on display, earning £35,000 of ticket sales in eight months. Attracting 10,000 people a day – including Lord Byron, who liked it so much that he had a copy made by a Long Acre coach maker (adding to the field-general's more perfunctory amenities a travelling library and dining facilities) – the carriage attracted more visitors than any previous London show.[16] By the time Bullock went on tour with it in August, 220,000 people had been to see it, including the cartoonists Cruikshank and Rowlandson. Of their caricatures of the subject, Thomas Rowlandson's is the most wittily demotic. Exuberant as a circus, it depicts a bunfight of fat-bottomed, voluptuously buxom, bonneted women ransacking the carriage and inspecting its fascinating domestic hardware, whilst fat-calved men in assorted hats and britches grope, poke and goose the women, or look on with lascivious amusement.

Rowlandson replicated Cruikshank's trademark profile of The Hottentot Venus among the Venus-bottomed women in the crowd, their bonnet plumes waving in homage to Saartjie-style millinery. One woman arches her back and plumps up her cape over her regrettably modest haunches better to

Satirical cartoon by Thomas Rowlandson depicting the exhibition of
Bonaparte's carriage at Bullock's Museum in 1816. A poster of Saartjie
Baartman is displayed next to Napoleon's bust and a playbill of popular
midget Count Boruwlaski.

accentuate her posterior attributes, Hottentot-Venus style, as
she waits to be lifted into the Emperor's coach. Rowlandson
draws the eye to the one ubiquitous difference between Saartjie
and the female crowd: she is in the naked array of nature,
while they are clothed with effortful artifice. On the wall
behind the riotous mob, between the banner for 'Bullock's
Museum of Natural Curiosities' and a scowling bust of the
conquered Napoleon, stands Saartjie, gaze averted from the
grovelling crowd. She pulls contemplatively on her pipe, her
buttocks loftily suspended above the human frenzy below.[17]

Pilloried in the English newspapers as a tyrannical ogre
since the turn of the century, Napoleon, like Saartjie, had had

his share of being misrepresented as an ugly, disfigured, savage and mesmerising immigrant. Most typically, he was caricatured as a pygmy with an enormous nose. The *Morning Post*, which followed the Hottentot Venus story so assiduously, described the Emperor as 'an unclassifiable being, half African, half European, a Mediterranean mulatto'.[18] By juxtaposing Saartjie and Napoleon in his cartoon, Rowlandson made a visual comment on two famous outsiders, and on the historical circumstance of the conjoining of the Baartman bottom and the Napoleonic bust.

Shortly after the allies took back Paris on 30 March 1814, Saartjie and Hendrik Cesars (the latter travelling under the rather feeble alias of Henry Taylor), boarded the mail coach to Dover, struck out seaward from under its chalk cliffs across the slate-grey channel and lumbered towards Paris into the eye of a historical storm.

Peering into the coach at the *barrière*, the uniformed soldiers saw, by the light of their flambeaus, the diminutive goddess of Eros wrapped in shawls up to her ears, cushioned by her stage kaross, her feet tucked up away from the damp, straw-strewn coach floor. Perhaps she returned a level stare, accompanied by a speculative chew of tobacco. Whatever had happened to Saartjie in the intervening period, she entered Paris without a child or a husband. Cesars adopted an alias because Lord Ellenborough's ruling had removed him from direct management of her, and the city was full of gossiping English. When Saartjie and Cesars arrived in Paris, slavery and the slave trade were still legal in France and her dominions.

Saartjie arrived in France in the wake of the final allied

effort against Napoleon. Newly bound by the Treaty of Chaumont,[19] brokered by Castlereagh, the allies, led by Tsar Alexander, took Paris on the last day of March. Napoleon abdicated four days later, Talleyrand led the vote in the French Senate for the return of the Bourbons, Louis XVIII was restored, and Napoleon left Fontainebleau for Elba.

Amid this tide of eminent men moving in and out of Paris was Georges-Léopold-Chrétien Cuvier, Europe's foremost scientist. As Saartjie's coach rolled into the city, the 'Mammoth', as he was nicknamed, dominated the National Museum of Natural History (Muséum National d'Histoire Naturelle), which was situated among the trees of the Jardin des Plantes. Comprising botanical gardens and an exotic zoo, the Jardin des Plants was presided over by Etienne Geoffroy Saint-Hilaire. Saartjie would soon be at the epicentre of the debate about race and the human species that raged between these two men, an intellectual battle described by Goethe as 'the most important event in European history'.[20]

Saartjie and Cesars took lodgings at 15 rue Neuve des Petits Champs (now the rue des Petits-Champs), parallel to the north end of the Palais Royal gardens, amid the terraced streets, glittering arcades and white colonnades of the Palais Royal,[21] Paris's theatre district and amusement mecca. Shop windows were as brightly lit as stage sets, and the glinting brass and swinging lamps of cafés, restaurants and theatre doors made the city centre a mirror endlessly reflecting its own glory. Everything shone brassily, infused with the energetically exhausted demob hysteria of the Restoration. Fifteen rue Neuve des Petit Champs had a well-known exhibition hall on the ground floor and accommodation above. The address had been home to many of the Palais Royal's leading attractions.

The streets of chic Paris teemed with strutting uniforms, frenzied fashions and a great competition of extravagant hats and bonnets that bobbed along the boulevards as if wearing their owners only in afterthought. Glass-fronted shop windows displayed 'natural' false teeth[22] and elaborate wigs. Spectral statues were poised motionless atop the thick forest of columns a few blocks away in the Jardin des Tuileries.[23] Blue mist rose off the Seine encircling the nearby Ile de la Cité, mingling with the cigarette smoke, pungent garlic, wine, brandy, coffee and hot-chocolate vapours drifting from the doorways of the many restaurants and cafés of the Palais Royal. Beyond the arc of artificial light illuminating the opulent bonnets and hats, plain blue cloth caps waited in the wings, sentries to the city's revolutionary future.

Situated at the heart of political Paris, the wrought-iron balconies of Saartjie's new home looked out over flagstones paved with Republican libertine tradition, a heady mixture of sex, knowledge, blood and freedom. Nearby, on the Left Bank, accessible via the Pont Neuf, the buildings of the Natural History Museum sat among the lush palms, pink flamingos and baying wolves of the Jardin des Plantes, recently renamed the Jardin du Roi following the defeat of Napoleon. The Natural History Museum, and the zoo and botanic gardens had been created out of the old medical school and royal medicines garden (Le Jardin du Roi) by the Revolutionary Convention in 1793.[24]

On 10 September, Professor André Thouin, the museum's administrator, received a letter from a certain Henry Taylor, containing an invitation to attend a private view at 15 rue Neuve des Petits Champs on the following Tuesday. Attached to the letter was a poster engraving. The original of the portrait, the letter explained, was a member of the 'Hottentot' tribe from the borders of the Gamtoos River in the African interior. Said woman was currently to be found in Paris, where she would shortly be shown. The letter stressed Saartjie's interest to the informed observer as an object of natural history. Before the public opening of the exhibition, Taylor offered an exclusive preview of this person and her *'conformation singulière'*[25] to the museum's professors.

This letter, read to the museum's weekly board meeting the day after the private view, was passed over in favour of a more urgent matter: the impending visit by the new Governor of the Cape, Lord Charles Henry Somerset. The board, composed of twelve professors, resolved to ask the new Governor for animals typical of South Africa to be added to their zoo. *'Peut-être un éléphant,'* the Mammoth is reported to have said,[26] pursuing his pet interest. Saint-Hilaire, Cuvier and Henri-Marie Ducrotay de Blainville were the board's leading members. As the intellectual descendents of Buffon, Lamarck and Linnaeus, they constituted the world's premier team of scientific naturalists. The board took no action on the letter from Mr Taylor, but Cuvier noted its contents in his legendary memory.[27]

Born in 1769, Cuvier had bright, penetrating blue eyes, thick red wavy hair, heavy-set features and a marked aptitude for self-preservation. He was short and wore the dishevelled clothing of the distracted dresser. Lean during the Revolutionary years, he filled out during the Empire, and after the Restoration 'grew enormously fat',[28] in consequence of which his walk was ponderous and cumbersome, and he avoided bending over, for fear of an attack of apoplexy.

By 1814, Cuvier held the Professorial Chair for

Comparative Anatomy at the Natural History Museum and the Chair of Natural History at the Collège de France, the world's largest scientific-research establishment. As thick-skinned as his elephantine namesake, he had risen to fame as Citizen Cuvier of the Revolutionary state, prospered under Napoleon as a member of the governing élite, and then inveigled himself into the good favour of the new monarchy with such a convincing, and newly revealed, display of anti-Revolutionary convictions as to be made Chancellor of the University of Paris, and Councillor of State to the King.

Despite hagiographic versions of Cuvier's career, he was in fact a plodding, assiduous creep and physical coward who owed his ascendance to the fact that he stayed firmly put and never took the adventurous risks involved in fieldwork, unlike his mentor, colleague and rival, Saint-Hilaire. Ultimately, Cuvier prevailed, but he was paranoid, lonely, self-piteous and constantly besieged by imaginary monsters threatening to assail his intellectual pre-eminence. For Saartjie, his primacy proved disastrous.

On Sunday, 18 September, Cesars placed an advertisement in the *Journal de Paris*, again under his pseudonym of Taylor, announcing the opening of his new exhibition:

The HOTTENTOT VENUS, recently arrived from London. Now on show to the public at 15, Rue Neuve des Petits Champs. This extraordinary phenomenon is the only member of the Hauzanana[29] [*sic*] tribe ever to have appeared in Europe. In this woman, as extraordinary as she is surprising, the public has a perfect example of this tribe, which inhabits the most southerly parts of Africa. The Hottentot Venus differs greatly in character

from her people, ordinarily most surly, in her sweetness, gracious-
ness and winning ways. She wears all those ornaments that on
holidays are used as ceremonial finery by the tribe to which she
belongs. One may obtain at the same place an engraving of the
Hottentot Venus, taken from life. Entry 3 fr.[30]

The paradox contained in this advertisement reveals something of Saartjie's intriguing allure; she is presented as 'a
perfect example' of her tribe while simultaneously differing
'greatly in character from her people'. Saartjie was marketed,
once again, as being both typical and unique. In fact she
captured the essence of contemporary Parisian entertainment: a compound of science, phantasmagoria, fantasy and
curiosity.

The announcement of Saartjie's first appearance in Paris
was listed under '*Spectacles*' and printed alongside a cornu-
copia of adverts for variety entertainments. London and
Paris shared a rage for panoramas; cosmoramas; mechanical demonstrations of new technology, such as 'Speaking
Machines' and 'Mechanical Trumpets'; séances and illusions. All of these were typical entertainments in the Palais
Royal. For 2 francs, coffee drinkers at the Café de Foy could
venture upstairs to view the *Alparama*, which offered a
three-dimensional journey through the 'Simplon Pass, the
Alps, the Jura, Ferney-Voltaire, etc.'[31] Panoramas were a
particular craze. These enormous painted postcards, usually
circular or semi-circular, offered the spectator the illusion
of instant transportation to foreign places, including natural
wonders and the conquering capitals of the allied forces.
Alongside the notice of The Hottentot Venus, audiences
were invited to visit just such an enormous walk-in

panorama, opposite the Louvre, on the rue de Rivoli. Visitors were promised a demonstration of 'mechanical effects'[32] followed by experiments in 'physics and phantasmagoria'.[33]

Saartjie was unknown when she arrived in London in 1810, but when she reached Paris in 1814 she was a recognised icon whose reputation as scantily clad totem goddess preceded her. Rumoured nudity, flaunted buttocks and curling pipe smoke had become her trademarks, and there was gossip that she was a courtesan or prostitute. These were stage fictions. She had never yet appeared naked on stage. Her bottom was, granted, impressive, but far from unusual in the mere fact of being substantial. The pipe was a prop. Saartjie must have dissipated many hours of boredom blowing smoke into the eyes of her fascinated audience, contemplating their spectacular idiocy and casual cruelty.

Now that she had only Cesars to look after, Saartjie's household duties were lighter. Each other's meal ticket, the duo were more than ever firmly bound by the mutual tyranny of master and servant. Yet earning their passage back to Cape Town appeared by this time to be more of an incentive to Cesars than to Saartjie.

In Paris Saartjie was transformed. She became overwhelmingly amiable and ebullient on stage, joking with her audience in Dutch and English.[34] She danced with energy, and her singing in 'her own mother-tongue' charmed the Parisian critics. This behaviour was ambiguous: was she genuinely cheerful, or was her jollity a mask for misery? Freed of Dunlop, she had a fuller share of her earnings and the novelty of a new, warmer, foreign city. Possibly she had a new lover; there were unsubstantiated press reports that she married in Paris. Yet her greater engagement with her audiences increased rather than reduced her aura of loneliness and isolation, and it suggested an increasingly cognac-fuelled desperation at the realisation that her circumstances were inescapable. Through her travels she had discovered the boundlessness of servitude for the poor and unfree.

Saartjie worked her six-hour shift noon till six, and spent the evenings in the restaurants, bars and cafés of the district drumming up business, or going by private invitation to 'charming'[35] houses to enliven dinners, parties[36] and salons. After a day of being ogled and prodded on the boards, she was subjected to the prurient curiosity of her European sisters, denizens of polite society. At one supper party in the Palais Royal, Saartjie's entrance into the plush room caused hysteria among the ladies, who rushed away from her, apparently terrified, 'and huddled behind the curtains'.[37] Observing this reaction, she was 'plunged into a sudden fit of melancholy'.[38] She bowed her head, and tears fell from her eyes. Her pathetic vulnerability reassured, perhaps even shamed, the cowering women. They ventured from behind the curtains and approached her, holding her hands, fingering her necklaces and touching her clothes.[39] Following so fast on their fear and rejection, the objectifying curiosity displayed in this sudden, uninvited physical intimacy must have been almost unendurable.

Satirists cast Saartjie in the role of Paris's favourite noble savage savant. Looking at Parisian society with an apparently natural outsider's eye, she was portrayed once again as the topical stranger, commenting with innocent wit on the excesses of Restoration society. The *Journal de Paris* ran two typical pieces in this vein. Penned by a journalist impersonating Saartjie, they purported to be letters written home to her cousin in South Africa, arbitrating on fashion and commenting on the manners of French and English women, and on the relations between the sexes.

On 19 November a one-act play entitled *The Hottentot Venus: or the Hatred of Frenchwomen* opened at the Vaudeville Theatre. Written by Messrs Théaulon de Lambert, Dartois and Brazier, with a score of no less than thirty-four musical numbers selected by Doche, the show borrowed the plot of Vadé's *Canadian Girl* and starred a popular young actress, Mlle Rivière. Adolphe, a young baronet-to-be and victim of two fickle French wives, inspired by traveller's tales, resolves to marry '*une femme sauvage*' on whom he can count to be free of civilised vices. He is encouraged in this plan by his uncle, the Baron, a bluff traveller who assures him that 'Frenchwomen are the most beautiful in the world, except for American Indian Squaws and Hottentot girls.'[40] Adolphe's cousin Amélie, secretly in love with him, dresses herself up 'in gorgeous Hottentot costume',[41] pretends to speak only untranslatable 'Hottentot' and inveigles the smitten Adolphe into a betrothal. Amélie is unmasked when a chevalier who is in love with her dramatically unrolls a print of the real Hottentot Venus, whose show he has just seen in Paris. At the sight of her portrait, 'everyone gives a cry of terror', and Adolphe's desire for a barbarian bride is instantly exorcised. He marries Amélie, and conventional white, heterosexual order is restored.[42]

The show was an instant box-office hit. Reviewers compared Mlle Rivière with Saartjie, disparaging the original: 'There is more than one difference between Mlle Rivière and her foreign model. A young and pretty actress like herself can have no relation to a *savage Venus*.'[43] Another wag seized the opportunity to experiment with the uses of Saartjie's image as pornography. Visiting 'Miss Sartjee' early in the morning, he found her sleepy and undressed:

> Ravished at such a fair sight I was tactful enough not to presume too long upon her indulgence: I let her pass into her apartments. To my own I then retired, and tried in vain to find Diversion in her image, all alone.[44]

French audiences both feared and adored Saartjie for her difference. It was an idolatrous kind of love, infused with unapologetic, intensely eroticised exoticism. 'When it comes to blacks, the imagination of white folks is something else,'[45] Josephine Baker would observe when treading the boards of Paris a century later. The original Hottentot Venus might have concurred.

In fact Saartjie was the first in a series of African Venuses to ascend the Parisian stage. In 1925, audiences would follow the scent of wonder created by her in 1814 directly to the floodlit façade of the Théâtre des Champs-Elysées, where Baker, newly arrived from Harlem, opened in *La Revue Nègre* with her *danse sauvage*. An unsettling combination of electrifying eroticism and comic burlesque, Baker took dance steps from St Louis and New York – 'the shake, the shimmy, the mess-around'[46] – and conquered Paris with a dance whose centre of gravity was her powerfully seductive belly and undulating buttocks. Jutting her bottom out, dropping to crawl and wiggle on her hands and knees, her neck and ankles trimmed with feathers, her hair cropped short, Baker's *danse sauvage* was an explicit homage to The Hottentot Venus that stirred memories of the unbridled sexuality and primitivism projected onto her voluptuous forebear.[47] Press reviews were embellished with the language of colonialist fantasy. Strikingly, the language used to describe the two women was almost identical. A century apart, both were cast as 'instinctive', 'exotic', 'primitive' and 'savage'.[48]

Saartjie's popular image in England was of wiliness, strongwilled belligerence and opportunism. The trial over her freedom concluded with her being chided for delinquency because she chose immoral earnings, but her media image remained that of a shrewd subcultural 'blackbird' full of practical ingenuity in the pursuit of turning a penny. In France, she metamorphosed into a tragic heroine and showgirl manqué, a fallen goddess of love, the epitome of the African exotic.

Despite the success of her show, Saartjie and Cesars struggled to cope with life in Paris. They spoke little French, and their contacts were poor. Cesars had promised his wife that he would return to South Africa after five years. His time was nearly up, but he had yet to make his fortune. At the end of October, he extended Saartjie's daily show times from six to a punishing ten hours, to maximise profits.[49] Performing daily from eleven in the morning to nine at night took its toll, and by the end of the year she was suffering from exhaustion, recurrent flu and the deleterious effects of the brandy she drank to keep going through her performances, private viewings, evening displays at cafés and restaurants, and attendance at late-night salons, parties and balls. Gradually, her ailments mutated into alcohol-related illnesses.

It is possible that Cesars drove her on with the incentive of raising sufficient funds for their joint passage home. Even if she believed him, the enticements for Saartjie to return were ambiguous. Going back to Cape Town meant that she could stop performing like a circus turn for insatiable European audiences but that she would have to take up her life as domestic servant in the Cesars household again. It wasn't much of a choice.

Buoyed up by the obsession of novelty-driven Paris with the Hottentot Venus phenomenon, takings were good in the run up to the end of 1814. But when the New Year began with Saartjie too ill to perform, Cesars panicked. He became churlish about the costs of all medicines except the supply of brandy that quieted her anxious remonstrations about the poor state of her health and how tired she was.

The eventful year of 1815 was calamitous for Saartjie. On the evening of 20 March, Napoleon re-entered Paris and was carried up the steps of the Tuileries by a frenzied crowd.[50] A frightened Louis XVIII had fled down the same steps the night before, on his way to Ghent. He would return, exactly one hundred days later, following Napoleon's defeat at Waterloo. By October, the former Republican Emperor would be banished to the mournful, storm beaten volcanic rock of St Helena, the prison island en route to Cape Town.

Two months earlier in January while Saartjie had been languishing in bed with flu, a predatory showman named Réaux, who had followed her success since her arrival in Paris, sensed opportunity and offered to take over *la Vénus hotten-tote* from Cesars. There is no record of the deal struck. Shortly thereafter Cesars returned to Cape Town. It is certain that he profited from the sale of Saartjie's exhibition rights; when he died in 1841, he left Anna Catharina a modest inheritance of 'two thousand ryks dollars pure'.[51] Revising their will in August of that year, the newly widowed Anna Catharina appointed Pieter Willem Cesars her universal heir, suggesting that their adopted daughter, Anna Catharina, had died or become estranged. Through this twist of fate, Pieter Willem Cesars, the man who had taken Saartjie from her home to Cape Town, inherited the remainder of the wealth earned from her exploitation.

Together for so long, Saartjie and Cesars parted company as swiftly as the turning of the tide. Saartjie was on her own, having learned too late the fundamentally Faustian law of show-business contracts. Her emotional distress at Cesars's departure was evident. Her characteristic stoicism crumbled, and she wept in public, began to describe herself to strangers as unfortunate, and drank more and more brandy.

Saartjie's return to the stage following her illness was announced on 22 January 1815[52] at a new venue on the rue Montesquieu, 'opposite the Baths'.[53] 'The Hottentot Venus has changed owner'[54] screamed press reports the following day, asserting, with no apparent basis in fact, that Réaux was also now her husband. Réaux was a shady figure. Described disingenuously in official correspondence with the Natural History Museum as merely 'a householder of Paris'[55] he was in fact an entertainer and animal trainer with close connections to the city's naturalists and scientists. He lived with his small menagerie at 7 Cour des Fontaines (now Place de Valois), a courtyard directly opposite the east side of the Jardin du Palais Royal, formerly the kitchens and laundry of the Palais Royal. It was to this address that Saartjie moved following Cesars's departure.

Monkey chatter, parrot squawks and a chorus of constant rustling and scratching could be heard in the cobbled courtyard outside Réaux's apartment windows. The scientists nearby at the Natural History Museum, keepers of their own much larger bestiary, feigned disinterest in Réaux's populist occupations, yet they knew him well, as he served as one of the museum's network of animal resurrectionists who, in exchange for cash, delivered small furry bodies in sacks for dissection and addition to the museum's growing natural-history collection.

Although Saartjie was barely recovered from her illness, Réaux reopened the Hottentot Venus exhibition with an extended show time, a gruelling twelve-hour shift from eleven in the morning until eleven at night. To promote the revival, he ran a daily press campaign for over a fortnight and announced new public perambulations of the Venus around Paris, for which he would give twenty-four hours' advance notice.[56]

Réaux also began to speculate on other means of earning revenue from Saartjie's display. Taking advantage of his connections with the Natural History Museum, Réaux hatched a ghastly scheme, suggested to him in passing by Cesars and consolidated by his own experience of selling animals to the keepers of the Jardin des Plantes. Without her consent, Réaux prepared the way for a performance that would make him a small fortune, and ultimately cost Saartjie her life.

Saartjie's desperation became increasingly evident. She was breaking down and crying uncontrollably in public. With nothing left to lose, she abandoned her reticence and told her story to anyone who would listen and could interpret her polyglot of Dutch, English, and a little, hesitant French. Apart from journalists hungry for a new angle on the Hottentot Venus phenomenon, few listened. When Saartjie did find a willing audience, she worried over the details of her childhood, returning constantly to the death of her father, the moment her home fell apart. Like many exiles fearing that they might never return to the land of their birth, she began to tell traveller's tales, piecing together memories of who she had been before leaving home. Only three days after her new show managed by Réaux opened, she threw herself upon the seemingly sympathetic journalist to whom she told her story in unprecedented detail.

Still so young, Saartjie's life had been dramatic and eventful. Throughout 1815, it was as if she was for the first time beginning to take stock of the journey she had made. Without Cesars, she had lost all continuity with her past and finally confronted the realisation that she might never return to South Africa. Increasingly world-weary, she was nostalgic for things she had never known.

9

PAINTED FROM THE NUDE

In the early spring of 1815, a few days after the news reached Paris that Napoleon was marching on the capital, Saartjie made her way through the verdant chestnut and plane-trees in the Jardin des Plantes on the Left Bank. By arrangement between Réaux and the professorial board of the Natural History Museum, she was on her way to pose for three days as a life model for a panel of scientists and artists.[1]

Prompted by Cesars's letter to the board, Cuvier went to see *la Vénus hottentote* perform and asked Réaux to arrange a meeting with Saartjie after the show.[2] The Mammoth was fascinated and talked with her at length, swiftly replenishing her quickly finished drinks. He recorded that she was cheerful and conversational and that she drank to excess.

The French scientific community had been following Saartjie's career since her show had opened. As recorded in the diary of Sir Charles Blagden,[3] during 1814 and 1815 the circle of savants based at the great chemist Claude-Louis Berthollet's country-house research institute at

Arcueil, just outside Paris, discussed Saartjie. Blagden, a physician who began his career as an army surgeon, was Secretary of the Royal Society and right-hand man to Sir Joseph Banks throughout the 1780s and '90s. In 1805, when Cuvier was made a Fellow of the Royal Society, Blagden was a signatory to his acceptance certificate. By 1814, he was in Paris and based at the Arcueil institute. The scientists gathered there worked on a shared research programme and formed a tight-knit community. The group included, among others, Alexander von Humboldt, the father of modern geology and geography; James Smithson, the founder of the Smithsonian Institution in Washington DC; and Dominique-François-Jean Arago, the physicist and astronomer who discovered the sun's chromosphere.

On 9 October 1814, these luminaries raised the subject of Saartjie at a dinner gathering. Blagden noted in his diary: 'Talk about the The Hottentot Venus, before the girls; kept within the bounds of decency.'[4] The comment speaks for itself as regards which of Saartjie's attributes were of most interest to the scientists. A further entry in January 1815 describes much discussion between these men about 'Hottentots' and the question of whether 'it's the Bosjeman women only who have the apron' and 'the large posteriors'.[5] Jean-Claude Mertrud, professor of comparative anatomy at the Natural History Museum and zoo, said that he much admired Cuvier's opinions on the subject.

Cuvier's protégé, Henri de Blainville, Assistant Professor at the Académie des Sciences, was also eager to scrutinise Saartjie. Saint-Hilaire and Cuvier took control of the arrangements. A panel was assembled comprising zoologists, naturalists, anatomists, physiologists, artists and draughtsmen. Leading the scientific group were the formidable triumvirate of Saint-Hilaire, Cuvier and De Blainville.

On 16 February, Saint-Hilaire wrote to Monsieur Boucheseiche, head of the Paris police, requesting authorisation to bring Saartjie to the Jardin du Roi for examination. Réaux, Saint-Hilaire assured Boucheseiche, had given undertakings to act with discretion to preserve the public order.[6] Réaux requested a report from the scientists, which he could use as further credentials for Saartjie's exhibition.

Saint-Hilaire, the youngest of the twelve founder-professors, held the chair of the Department of Quadrupeds, Cetaceans, Birds, Reptiles and Fish at the Natural History Museum and Jardin des Plantes. Dedicated to scientific research and teaching, the extensive, well-resourced museum was the pre-eminent institution in the Enlightenment pursuit of modern science throughout Europe, and the epicentre of the study of the life sciences.[7]

The Jardin des Plantes was the world's first and biggest municipal institution of its kind.[8] When Saartjie passed through it on her way to being examined, drawn and painted by the foremost natural scientists of Europe, it had glass animal houses and iron railings enclosing wild cats, lions, monkeys, baboons, buck, ostriches, rhinoceroses and a pair of elephants.[9] Several of the animals, such as the zebra and gnu, were gifts from governors of the Cape.[10] There was a bear pit, a pergola of pink flamingos, and trees filled with chattering wood-pigeons, red-chested cuckoos, chorister robins and sugarbirds. The aloes, cacti and frangipanis were comfortingly familiar to Saartjie, reminiscent as they were of home. For native Parisians they were strange new species and took on a fecund lustre and alien mystery in their new urban habitat.[11]

Standing on a platform in the atelier, her arm resting on a chair, Saartjie looked down at the men, their eyes sharp and bright with curiosity, looking up at her from a 'steatopygous' perspective.[12] Notebooks, sketchbooks, inkstands, pens, pins, charcoal, eyeglasses and a host of strange instruments bestrewed the lamplit room. Stoves burned off the chill of the spring morning.

Cuvier, De Blainville and Saint-Hilaire led the scientific team. All three specialised in comparative anatomy and zoology. A sort of early nineteenth-century Indiana Jones, Saint-Hilaire had enthusiastically joined Napoleon's Egyptian campaign and enjoyed three years of high-risk scientific adventures amid the Pyramids, collecting skulls and artefacts, studying the crocodiles of the Nile, and pursuing his fascination with the ancient art of snake-charming. During his absence, Cuvier, eschewing boy's own adventures and sensing professional opportunity, superseded Saint-Hilaire as France's leading naturalist. On his return, Saint-Hilaire developed his research on genetic exaggerations and comparative embryology. Contesting the notion that physical freakery was a quirk of fate, he argued that such aberrations explained normal development. In so doing, he founded the science of teratology: the study of monstrosities or abnormal formations in animals and plants.[13]

The other members present from the Académie des Sciences included the physiologist Pierre Flourens and Cuvier's brother Frédéric, Keeper of the Menagerie. Cuvier's research assistants Simon-Pierre Rousseau and Charles-

Léopold Laurillard were on hand to help and to provide Saartjie with refreshments.

The museum had its own in-house team of staff painters. Resident artist Léon de Wailly's career demonstrates the intimate relationship between art and science in the period.[14] Professor of Drawing at the Conservatoire Royal des Arts et des Métiers, De Wailly was appointed to the museum in 1803. Specialising in quadrupeds and birds, he painted for the museum's visual archive those living animals 'where no likeness exists'.[15] Nicolas Huet and Jean-Baptiste Berré produced hundreds of watercolour illustrations of flora and fauna, as well as anatomical drawings for the museum's professors, working alongside the famous Redouté brothers, whose delicate drawings were regarded as the pinnacle of botanical illustration and flower painting. The work of Huet, De Wailly and Berré was both integral to the scientific project and collectible popular art. Colour prints and posters of their work were reproduced and sold in great quantity all over Paris, and their illustrations of new exotica at the zoo were particularly appealing to the general public.

None of these artists, however, usually painted human subjects.

On the first day of her examination, Saartjie arrived in her stage costume, as she believed the occasion required. Getting togged up in this outfit took some considerable effort, yet as Saartjie arranged herself for the viewing, the men around her seemed disconcerted. The source of their dissatisfaction soon became clear. They expected her to pose naked. A battle ensued in which Saartjie, object of the moment, attempted heroically to hold her ground. She argued with them, ignored their entreaties and refused to remove a single item of her ensemble.

Henri de Blainville made it clear that the scientists, anatomists, physiologists and artists gathered to examine *la Vénus hottentote* distanced themselves, as intellectual men of art and science, from any interest in Saartjie's personality and talents:

As for what she had clearly learnt from Europeans, in order to exercise her trade, such as dancing . . . accompanying herself with skill on the tambourine, playing the Jew's harp, making certain gestures which one supposed to be of prayer, or her numerous and hideous grimaces . . . this [is] of little interest to naturalists.[16]

The disdain of the scientists towards Saartjie's artistic abilities and commercial assets could not have been plainer. And De Blainville's dismissive suggestion that she merely mimicked her cultural accomplishments 'from Europeans' was a cultural and racial insult.

What intrigued Saartjie's surveyors was the prospect of a close-up view of the legendary somatic attributes of Khoisan women. In five years of public performance, Saartjie had never appeared nude. Always covered by her skin-coloured fleshings, her fur-trimmed silk-stockinged body had suggested without revealing, deforming the dreams of viewers, and stimulating the curiosity and prurient surmise of those who had seen her, in person or in print. Whether she was physical fact or theatrical fiction was a mystery popular audiences had to decide for themselves. Such theatrical ambiguity was, however, anathema to the modern scientific classifiers of the world. Self-appointed arbiters of the imagination, they would discover what was fact about Saartjie Baartman and in the process vanquish fiction. For them to achieve this objective, they needed The Hottentot Venus to be naked. Ribbons, feathers, beads, stockings, fur cape, headdress, carefully applied make-up, musical instruments, accessories, intimate garments. Everything but her chewing tobacco and pipe had to go.

Saartjie was furious and appalled. The examination, formulated as an exercise in controlled scientific objectivity, was held up by protracted negotiations over her stubborn unwillingness to undress. By dint of courteous modesty, she had found a way to subvert the proceedings. The extent to which her attitude affected the entire event is reflected in De Blainville and Cuvier's scientific lectures. Both men were forced to dedicate a large part of their research papers to the very unscientific subject of describing the problems caused by Saartjie's intractability on the point of removing her clothes.

* * *

'La Vénus Hottentote', cartoon by George Loftus, Paris, 1814.

In classical legend Venus dominated hearts and minds largely by means of her famous girdle. Imbued with mystical powers, this unique raiment had the power to excite love and rekindle passion, and granted beauty, grace and elegance when worn even by the most deformed.[17] This accessory enabled Juno to gain the attentions of Jupiter, and helped Venus to subdue Vulcan's jealousy of her manifold infidelities. Elaborating on this theme, European travellers to South Africa attributed to Khoisan women the legendary 'Hottentot apron', a pinny of flesh supposed to conceal the 'Hottentot' female's *mons Veneris*. While Greek goddesses wore magical detachable corsetry, nobly savage Venuses, subdued to servitude, had – according to travellers' accounts – natural 'aprons' concealing their fecund genitalia and emphasising their unique and alien appearance. This speculation set up a notion of natural, feminised subordination, at the same time eroticising that subjection.

Many European male travellers colluded in this collective fantasy, and a debate raged for 250 years as to whether the legendary 'Hottentot apron' resulted from nature or culture. When Captain Cook stopped at Cape Town on his way home in March 1771, he confided to his diary that he intended to use the opportunity to explore 'the great question among natural historians, whether the women of this country have or have not that fleshy flap or apron which has been called the *Sinus pudoris*'.[18] Those favouring the natural explanation dubbed the supposed condition with a pseudo-scientific description – hypertrophy of the *labia minora* – and seized on the apron as the clinching evidence that South Africa's much-debated indigenous people were in fact fundamentally a different species to Europeans. It was only a short, diabolical step from there to positing that 'Hottentots' were the missing link in the chain of being between humans and animals, and therefore essentially bestial in nature.

Others disagreed, arguing for the notional Hottentot *tablier* as a form of cultural genital manipulation best understood as a fashion, designed (depending on the commentator) to stimulate or repel erotic desire. As early as 1640, Nicolaus de Graaf described the resulting bodily 'ornament' as 'short thongs hanging down, cut from the body'.[19] François Le Vaillant, friend of Cuvier and fellow member of the Société des Observateurs de l'Homme (the world's first anthropological society), determined to recast the 'Hottentot' as Africa's noble savage, also proposed a cultural explanation for the 'famous apron'.[20] It was, Le Vaillant claimed with paternalistic indulgence, a rather excessive, absurd foible of body-modification fashion, designed to modestly cover women's genitals and neutralise desire.[21]

Cuvier and De Blainville were thoroughly versed in these debates. Cuvier was a founder-member of the Société des Observateurs de l'Homme, established in 1799 by Louis-François Jauffret. Other biologists among the founding group included Lamarck, Antoine de Jussieu and Saint-Hilaire; the explorers Bougainville and François Le Vaillant; and the linguists Antoine Destutt de Tracy and Henri Sicard.[22]

Using first-hand reports from their friends and historical travel accounts, the scientists at the Natural History Musum hoped to discover for themselves the nature of this mantle of modesty. There was a typical colonial contradiction about black female sexuality at the heart of how travellers and scientists imagined the 'Hottentot apron'. It was seen to signify the notion that Khoisan women were simultaneously uncontrollably libidinous and coyly modest. Whether a result of nature or nurture, the apron, it was believed, functioned to conceal and contain excessive sexuality and deviant desires. In time-honoured tradition, the virgin and the whore were rolled into one.

But Saartjie had neither a magical girdle nor a 'Hottentot apron'. She had only a handkerchief.

It was the Mammoth who finally persuaded her to remove her clothes. He and De Blainville competed to secure this concession. Saartjie's body became the territory battled over in their escalating struggle for pre-eminence. Furious, miserable and exposed, she sought to retain her dignity with her little handkerchief.

Mindful of modern accounts, especially Le Vaillant's influential *Voyages*, De Blainville remained unconvinced by Réaux's salacious claim that Saartjie was a nymphomaniac who had on at least one occasion seen fit to 'threw herself upon a man she desired'.[23] De Blainville found her gentle and shy, charming when she liked someone, stubborn and contrary when she did not. Her modesty and evident dislike of him proved great obstacles to his scientific enterprise:

> She appears to know shame, or there was at least a great deal of difficulty in persuading her to allow herself to be seen naked, and she was almost unwilling to discard, for a moment, the handkerchief with which she hid her sexual organs. All the more then, was it impossible to obtain permission from her to make an adequate examination of them.[24]

Exasperated, De Blainville resorted to barefaced bribery. Saartjie, offended, refused. Much to Cuvier's satisfaction and amusement, she 'conceived a kind of hatred for M. de Blainville'.[25] In addition to his pestering, De Blainville made himself look ridiculous to Saartjie by the contorted positions he assumed in his attempts to try and find empirical evidence of her 'Hottentot apron'. By his own account, his acrobatics made him look ludicrous:

> In ordinary position, that is to say in upright posture, one certainly sees no sign of any kind of pedicule formed by the *labia majora*, such as may be seen in the illustrations of Messrs Peron and Le Sueur, and even less any projection of the *labia minora*; but in certain positions, as for example when Saartjie bent down, or even when she walked, on looking from behind one could see hanging between the thighs a fleshy appendage of at least an inch in length, which [I] supposed to be most likely nothing other than the *labia minora*, which [I] could not however say with certainty.[26]

De Blainville was disappointed. Saartjie's genitals appeared to be ordinary in appearance and dimension, much the same as the sexual parts of European women whom he knew more intimately. Frustrated, he decided to ignore the empirical evidence and lean his conclusions on travel accounts:

> . . . as to whether what was unusual in the bodily organisation of this woman derived from a natural disposition of the Hottentot race, or was the result of a pathological state . . . it was easy for him to show, on the basis of reports by the best travellers, from Barrow especially, that the form of the head

and the jaws is constant in the race, the extraordinary enlargement of the buttocks and the prolongation of the *labia minora* also being natural to it, but only achieving their greatest development with age, and more particularly with pregnancy.[27]

With a final misogynistic flourish, De Blainville concluded that Saartjie's *labia minora* would have been more visibly pronounced had she been older or pregnant.

Cuvier's approach was different. He advanced gently on Saartjie and won her over with a chilling, caddish courtesy. 'She was,' he said like a gallant, 'good enough to undress and allow herself to be painted from the nude.'[28]

Resolute in her strategic placement of the carefully negotiated handkerchief, Saartjie posed before the scientists and artists in unmistakable imitation of Botticelli's Venus rising from the sea, her auburn tresses cupped to conceal her vagina behind her hand. Scientists and Latinists would have observed an anatomical quip: the mount of Venus is the pad of fat at the base of the thumb as well as the elevation on the *mons Veneris*.

After Saartjie's three days of life-modelling, Berré, Huet and De Wailly had produced a series of paintings that became her most enduring and famous portraits. In 2002, De Wailly's likeness was chosen by the South African government as her official national image. These paintings were intended to join the flora and fauna collections in the library of the Natural History Museum, as well as provide illustrations for the scientists' own publications.

Huet depicted Saartjie in stark, anatomically defined profile, emphasising her buttocks. In terms of the Platonic assertion that there are two Venuses, one celestial, the other vulgar,[29]

Portrait by Nicolas Huet, Paris, March 1815.

Huet's image is a realist *Venus naturalis.* Far from outlandish or unfamiliar to the Western eye, the evolving conventions of the female nude in European art are apparent in this image.

De Wailly's portrait positions Saartjie standing in an undulating landscape. De Wailly's gentle rendering of Saartjie's face suggests that he felt some compassion towards her. Her troubled eyes gaze back at the viewer with an expression of deep sadness.[30] Her eyes draw attention away from her nudity, and, as with all the best portraiture, create in the viewer the illusion of being directly looked at, and challenged. De Wailly's Saartjie stands in the antique pose of the Cnidian Venus, so beloved of Renaissance sculptors; this figure would reappear later in the nineteenth century in the Orientalist *grandes odalisques* of Ingres and Renoir. Berré's paintings show Saartjie from five perspectives, and his rendering of her face is the most romantic. Her softly curled hair frames a smiling face, lips slightly parted to reveal a seductive flash of teeth. This image was produced in two versions, one with Saartjie naked, one in a luridly pink tasselled mini-apron. Berré's painted engraving was used to illustrate De Blainville's lecture on Saartjie when it was first published in a scientific journal in 1816.[31] In this image, De Blainville's invented elongated *labia minora* hang suspended from Saartjie's neatly trimmed pubic *mons Veneris* and tucked coyly between her thighs, a visual lie to support De Blainville's specious argument. Having never got behind the handkerchief, De Blainville simply invented fabulous, swinging pudenda in his feverish imagination. Outside the picture, beneath Saartjie's feet, lies a detailed and pornographically explicit cartouche of a vagina. Its labia are depicted as wings taking off beneath a

Portrait by Jean-Baptiste Berré Paris, March 1815.

Coloured engraving and genital cartouche of Jean-Baptiste Berré's original, published in 1816 in the *Journal Complémentaire du Dictionnaire des Sciences Médicales*

soft pile of pubic hair, the whole framing the smooth, dark cherry of an engorged clitoris, underneath which the white aperture of the vagina glints in a suggestive smile.

Significantly, it is only between the élite covers of the *Bulletin des Sciences par la Société Philomathique* that Berré's image appears in this explicit form of scientific peep-show erotica. Elsewhere, a highly ornate, brightly painted girdle has been added, tied around Saartjie's waist, a suggestive fringe concealing her *mons Veneris*. Thus exactly the same image was used to represent the opposing views of the secret of the 'Hottentot apron' as natural pathology of the body and as cultural fashion accessory.

Cuvier, Saartjie noticed, went out of his way to disarm her. As many models before her discovered, life-modelling was boring, uncomfortable and tiring. She shifted on her plinth, longing to stretch the stiff arm that held her handkerchief to her never fully revealed genitals. Cuvier tried to signal his difference from the other men. Apparently ignoring the anomalous situation, he coaxed Saartjie with chivalry, as if at a soirée where gentlemanliness required him to be solicitous of her needs. He personally offered her refreshments, requested her compliance with quiet courtesy and made little jokes which made her laugh in spite of herself.[32] All of this disarming behaviour concealed Cuvier's true intentions. In her presence for three entire days, he conceived a passion for Saartjie that would not be satisfied until he possessed her completely.

Cuvier's fascination became a morbid, deeply eroticised obsession. His objectifying scientific gaze was indistinguishable from sexual curiosity, the compulsions of desire and the intense erotic charge of physical difference that she awakened in him. Through this most famous Venus the scientist enacted his rage[33] against all women, whom he regarded as excessive, fecund and untrustworthy creatures whose natural reproductive abilities exceeded his strenuous, god-like attempts to name, order, classify and thus subdue the world around him.

On 18 March, only a few days after Saartjie had gone to the museum to be drawn, De Blainville delivered the first draft of his paper, entitled 'On a Woman of the Hottentot Race', to the Société Philomathique. Two days later Napoleon re-entered Paris. Nine days after his return, on 29 March, France once again abolished the slave trade.

10

THE DEATH OF VENUS

Saartjie never fully recovered from her severe illness of the winter of 1814. While the iconic status of *la Vénus hotten-tote* strengthened, the real Saartjie languished and weakened, from overwork, alcohol and loss of hope. Réaux no longer pressurised her to perform regularly. Increasingly reclusive, Saartjie withdrew into a rapid, painful decline. She had played out her last season on the Parisian stage, and her fame was now the reflected light of a dying star.

Without the daily routine of her show, Saartjie became listless. Increasingly, she went out only after dark, to enter-tain the beau monde at private audiences or to wander in the anonymity of the night in the nearby Palais Royal gardens. Her health was failing, and she needed alcohol, her only reassurance and constant companion in her disinte-grating world. Into this void, Réaux poured more and more of the spirits she demanded. He never denied her drink.

Brandy – *eau-de-vie* – stimulated Saartjie's enervated body and spirit, suffusing her with warmth. *Eau-de-vie*, the 'water of life', was also the agent that the scientists at the

Natural History Museum used as embalming fluid for their specimens. Formaldehyde, which was to provide scientists with more stable formalin solutions, was not introduced until 1893. Until then, potentially volatile spirits of alcohol were employed as both fixative and preservative for all human and animal tissue.[1] Cuvier had noted Saartjie's preference for *eau de vie*, commenting when he met her for the second time that 'what pleased her more than anything else was spirits.'[2]

It has been claimed that Saartjie became a prostitute towards the end of her life. While there is no documented evidence for this, it is possible that Réaux pimped her to selected clients. Her decline has also been mythologised as that of a decomposing Venus suppurating with smallpox and syphilis. However, these fictions owe more to the iconic imagery of the dying prostitute in nineteenth-century literature than to verifiable fact.

Saartjie was aware that Réaux watched her closely, as if weighing the meat on her bones, measuring her failing resistance to illness. The events at the Jardin du Roi (now restored to its republican name, the Jardin des Plantes) made it apparent to Réaux that Saartjie was now probably worth more to him dead than alive.

The professorial board had discreetly indicated their interest to Réaux following Saartjie's appearance before them. Should she happen to die, they would be pleased to pay a sum of money for the delivery of her corpse for the purposes of anatomical dissection. Such highly secretive arrangements had long been common practice among keepers of theatrical wonders, surgeons and anatomists. Frequently, the future donor was directly involved in the business agreement, indemnified with the benefits of much-needed cash for the remainder of their life in exchange for their consent to donate their corpses to science.[3] Réaux had done well out of Saartjie's live exhibition. Now he could capitalise on her death.

Saartjie slipped away, the last months of her life lost to a succession of illnesses. Repeated attacks of flu and bronchitis, lack of proper medical care, and excessive drinking left her vulnerable to respiratory disease. Réaux saw to it that alcohol was the only palliative to which she had access.

The winter of 1815 was bitterly cold and harsh. Saartjie died at 7 cour des Fontaines during the night of Friday, 29 December. Réaux did not call a priest. That is all we know.

In the icy dawn of Saturday, 30 December, Réaux left 7 cour des Fontaines, walking briskly over the Pont Neuf and along the Left Bank towards the Jardin des Plantes. The law required that deaths be declared immediately at the Mairie. Réaux, however, was walking resolutely in the wrong direction, to the homes of Saint-Hilaire and Cuvier, who lived in the grounds of the Natural History Museum.

Awoken by Réaux, with whom he had a hurried conference, Saint-Hilaire immediately wrote two urgent letters. First, a familiar note to the mayor – 'Monsieur et ami' – whom he notified of the death of *la Vénus hottentote*. Réaux, he slyly informed the mayor, was on his way to register her death officially with the municipal authorities. In the meantime, Saint-Hilaire was writing to give the mayor advance warning of his intention to remove Saartjie's body to the museum's anatomy laboratories, 'in the interests of the progress of human knowledge'.[4]

Next, Saint-Hilaire wrote to the Comte Anglès, Minister of State and Prefect of Police, requesting permission to take Saartjie's body to the museum:

Dear Sir

A woman of the Kaffir country shown by Mr Réaux under the name of the VENUS HOTTENTOT has just died in the Cour des Fontaines. This opportunity to acquire new information on this singular race of the human species leads us to ask you for permission for the body of this woman to be transported to the Anatomy Laboratory of the Natural History Museum.

My colleague Mr Cuvier, who is responsible at the museum for the teaching of comparative anatomy, begs me to assure you that he will see that all measures required by decency and appropriate to the circumstances should be rigorously implemented in the interest of public order.[5]

The Natural History Museum was not officially permitted to receive bodies for educational or scientific purposes. A decree of 1813 authorised dissection only at the medical faculty of the university of Paris and the Petie hospital. According to this directive, remains should be taken to the Clamart cemetery for proper burial after dissection. The Natural History Museum therefore had no legal right to dissect Saartjie.[6] Saint-Hilaire was asking the chief of police to bend the law. He obliged, authorising 'Sarjee's' corpse to be moved to the museum, assuming that Saint-Hilaire would be

(1) taking the necessary measures to preserve decency and

(2) co-ordinating for these purposes with the Commissioner of Police for the Palais Royal district, who [would] draw up an official minute recording the handover of the body.[7]

Before the Parisian *boulangers* had even finished baking their second batch of bread for the day, this process had been completed. Less than twenty-four hours after her death, without the solemnising of any rites, Saartjie's body was delivered to the Natural History Museum. Two documents were found carefully folded among her personal possessions: a copy of her contract with Dunlop, and her 1811 baptismal certificate. Réaux handed them over with her corpse. Among her remaining effects was a crumpled handkerchief.

Night closed in around the firmly secured shutters of the anatomical laboratory in the Jardin des Plantes. Inside, the dissection of The Hottentot Venus was underway. At the centre of the proceedings, the steely hearted Cuvier with his knives and saws concentrated deeply, cutting into Saartjie, naked, on her back on his anatomy bench. Her tortoiseshell pendant had been removed from her neck. Cuvier had finally got what he desired: Saartjie horizontal, unresisting, under his knife.

Cuvier's assistants bustled around the laboratory, helping at the bench, clearing blood and laying out perishable organs.

Others checked the setting of the plaster body casts taken directly from Saartjie's cadaver. Lard and plant oil were stirred into the viscous, boiling solution of Chinese wax to keep it the right consistency for taking moulds of her soft-tissued organs. Large glass bell-jars were set out on a workbench alongside flagons of distilled alcohol and potassium hydroxide, as if in preparation for the mixing of a cocktail for a giant. The bell-jars and *eau-de-vie* were for the preservation of Saartjie's brain and genitals, the potassium hydroxide for the boiling of her bones. Cuvier, with his habit of domesticating his science, always referred to this chemical compound by its more homely name of caustic potash.

By Monday morning, Cuvier and his team had completed the critical preliminary work on Saartjie's corpse. Plaster casts had been taken of her body. Once the whole figure was integrated, 'sculptors and artists finished the lines to the mould, polished the model surface with oil of turpentine, and then skin, vessels and body surface were painted on; the whole covered in a coat of clear varnish.'

Cuvier performed a post-mortem examination and full dissection, concluding with the removal of the brain. He sliced Saartjie's flesh around her hairline, peeled back her face, sawed through her cranium, removed her brain and embalmed it in *eau-de-vie*. Thirty-eight years later, Pierre Gratiolet would study this specimen.[8] In 1864 Professor Thomas Henry Huxley would cite Gratiolet's work on Saartjie's brain in a lecture that argued in favour of 'Negro' emancipation from slavery in America.[9]

Cuvier, however, was more interested in Saartjie's labia, clitoris, vagina and buttocks than her brain. Her genital organs were modelled in wax and the originals stoppered in a glass bell-jar awash with *eau-de-vie*. Cuvier thus secured himself both dry and wet preparations of his Venus's genitalia.[10]

The long labour of casting and dissection completed, Cuvier ordered the cleaning of the bloody laboratory and supervised the disarticulation of Saartjie's skeleton, taking immense care with its preparation. An 'entire skeleton'[11] is a thing 'infinitely precious',[12] Cuvier once said, referring to the difficulty of obtaining them for comparative anatomy. Cuvier described his method in the instructions he issued to his more adventurous colleagues in the anthropological society regarding how to collect skeletons on their travels. While he himself stayed in Paris, Saint-Hilaire, De Bougainville and Le Vaillant set out around the world with the following directions on how to collect human remains for Cuvier's lab studies. If voyagers saw or took part in 'battles with savages',[13] they were to make every effort to find 'the places where the dead are deposited' and obtain skeletons 'in any manner whatever'.[14] Each skeleton, Cuvier explained,

> should be boiled in caustic potash for several hours to remove the flesh, after which the bones were to be put in a bag, labelled and sent back to Europe where they might be reassembled. It would also be desirable to bring back some skulls with the flesh still intact. One had only to soak them in a solution of corrosive sublimate, set them out to dry, and they would become as hard as wood, their facial forms preserved without attracting insects. True, the sailors might oppose all this as barbarous, but the leaders must remember that a scientific expedition should be governed only by reason.[15]

What luck for the timid, travel-wary Cuvier. No need to do battle with savages, seek out umbrageous burial-grounds, stoke boiling cauldrons to strip human bones, or fear offending the sensibilities of sailors. His Hottentot Venus had come directly to his doorstep in the heart of Paris.

News of Saartjie's death made the Saturday papers. The *Journal général de France* claimed that The Hottentot Venus had 'died at 7 o'clock this morning, after a short illness of three days',[16] and reported as follows: 'It is said that the professors of the Museum of Natural History have asked that the body of this woman be placed at their disposal.'[17] '*La Vénus hottentote est morte*,'[18] announced Saartjie's obituary in *La Quotidienne* on New Year's Day. On Monday, 1 January, the *Annales Politiques, Morales et Litteraires* informed their readers of Saartjie's dissection. This potpourri of prejudice, racial condescension and ethnographic myth typifies the many articles published immediately following Saartjie's death:

> Just now, in one of the rooms of the Museum of Natural History, they are busy taking a mould of the Hottentot Venus, who died on the day before yesterday of an ataxic fever [a type of syphilis of the nervous system] that lasted only three days. Her body bears no visible traces of this illness except for a few brownish red spots around the mouth, on the thighs and the small of the back. Her general plumpness and her enormous protuberances are not diminished, and her extremely frizzy hair has not at all lengthened, as is ordinarily the case in Negroes during illness or after death. The dissection of this woman will provide M. Cuvier with an extremely curious

chapter for his account of the varieties of the human species. *The Hottentot Venus* provided the subject for plays and caricatures; she will now be the subject only of the naturalist's scalpel, and afterwards certain material parts of this divinity will have no other Olympus than a glass jar.[19]

So famed were Saartjie's 'enormous protuberances' that they needed no specification.[20]

A prescient letter written shortly after her show had opened in London in October 1811 anticipated the fear that resurrection men would haul off Saartjie's body for science, as well as reminding readers that she had laboured with poor health since her first winter in London:

Mr Editor

Having been one among the numerous visitors to that poor outcast of our species which is exhibited in Piccadilly, under the insulting appellation of the Hottentot Venus, I cannot help feeling myself considerably interested in behalf of a fellow creature in so helpless, friendless, and unpitied a condition.

My compassion has been further excited, by hearing it intimated that she would be a great anatomical curiosity, and that it is almost impossible that she should outlive the Winter in this country.

Not doubting that the feelings of the Public in this subject would be in unison with my own, and congenial to the religion we profess, and the laws under which we have the happiness to live, yet knowing something of the adventurous hardihood of science, I shall be extremely thankful if you will allow me, through your widely circulating publication, to express my hope that there is no possible connection between those two propositions.[21]

The anonymous author, 'A Man and A Christian', had hoped in vain.

Further obituaries followed, propagating the rumour that Saartjie had died of smallpox. The *Journal général de France* berated Réaux for his 'mindless obstinacy'[22] in not following advice 'to have his monster vaccinated'.[23] Using Saartjie's death as an opportunity to comment on the virulence of smallpox in the winter of 1816, the piece vaunted Edward Jenner's smallpox vaccine as 'the greatest discovery of which medicine may boast'.[24] The *Mercure de France* huffed, 'What proves that the Hottentot Venus wasn't really acclimatised is that she died of the *smallpox*. Our European Venuses would never have died of such a bagatelle.'[25]

Cuvier's conclusion on the cause of Saartjie's death was that she expired from an unspecified 'eruptive and inflammatory disease' ('*maladie inflammatoire et éruptive*').[26] Extrapolating from this, it has been suggested that she died from one or a combination of the following: pneumonia, pleurisy, smallpox and syphilis. However, the claim that she was carried off by the 'French pox' – i.e. syphilis – reflected popular prejudice, not medical fact. Overtly erotic women, both black and white, most especially showgirls, prostitutes and professionally exhibited 'freaks', were suspected of pathologically polluted sexuality. Their barely contained so-called 'primitive' subcutaneous desires might erupt at any moment through their excessive fleshliness.[27] The notion of Saartjie as venal Venus decomposing from the pox[28] would within a few decades make her the pre-eminent icon of atavistic sexuality in nineteenth-century European art and literature, from Zola to Baudelaire, Manet to Picasso.[29] These legends took root in the immediate wake of her untimely death.

Assertions that Saartjie died of smallpox ignored the already well-known dangers of handling a pustulent cadaver and overlooked the fact that the body casts show none of the chancrous disfigurations associated with death from this disease. Saartjie's death masks heartbreakingly show that her face was painfully swollen and her eyes puffy as she died. These symptoms do not prove smallpox, and are equally consistent with alcoholism and fatal pneumonia. The unproven possibility remains that she died from syphilis of the nervous system, known medically as locomotor ataxia or *tabes dorsalis*. It was this surmise that led to later claims that Saartjie died a penniless prostitute.

Cuvier's opinion was that it was probably *eau-de-vie* that finally carried Saartjie off. 'Her death might even be attributed to the excessive drinking in which she indulged during her last illness,'[30] he wrote, deploying the standard qualifier typical of many post-mortem reports. In other words, her last illness was not inevitably life-threatening, but her alcoholism prevented her body from fighting this final pathogenic onslaught.

Oddly enough, Saartjie's death coincided with the repatriation to Italy of the famous Roman statue known as the Medici Venus. 'Nothing but loss for ideal beauty'[31] was the laconic remark of the diarist of *L'Ambigu*, a journal published by a Frenchman in London and sold in both capitals: '. . .

the artists no longer have their *Venus alba*, but it is the naturalists who have got hold of the *Venus nigra*.'[32] Plundered from the Palazzo Uffizi by Napoleon, the celebrated Hellenistic statue[33] had arrived in Paris in 1802 after a ten-month journey by bullock cart.[34] At the end of December 1815, it was crated up and sent back to Florence. The English press was much taken with this coincidence. Fleet Street, predictably, went for the bottom line:

> The *Venus of Medicis* scarcely has flown,
> When Paris, alas! Your next Venus is gone;
> And no end to your losses you find:
> Well may you in sackcloth and ashes deplore;
> For the *former* fair form had no equal *before*,
> And the latter no equal *behind*.[35]

From the day after she died, Saartjie's unburied relics remained close to Cuvier until his own death and dissection. His apartments at the Natural History Museum opened directly onto the upper floor of his famous Cabinet d'Anatomie Comparée by way of an interconnecting mirrored door. The Lancastrian comparative anatomist Richard Owen (who coined the term *dinosauria* to describe giant extinct reptiles) visited the museum in 1822 and reported that the bell-jars containing Saartjie's brain and genitals were kept directly outside the door to Cuvier's private apartments.[36] These specimens, Owen stated, were preserved in 'bottles of a rude shape' without feet and made from 'common greenish glass'. The preparations were 'dropped in without any mode of suspension' and 'dimly visible through the dirty spirit'.[37] When required for demonstration or study, the organs were decanted. This French method, Owen explained, was more successful than the English practice of permanently sealing specimens, because it solved the perennial problem of how to prevent evaporation; every time the specimens were used, they were simply rebottled, and the jars topped up with alcohol and resealed.

Saartjie's skeleton was also in Cuvier's upper gallery, among 1,599 others, 41 of which were human, 'of the various races'.[38] These included three Egyptian mummies, the so-called Assassin of Kleber, an Italian with an extra lumbar vertebra, and eleven other 'Negroes or Hottentots'. Later these were joined by the skeleton of Bébé the dwarf, who had belonged to the deposed Polish King Stanislas, and a wax model of Supiot, a woman whose bones were 'all softened and twisted'.[39]

A whole apartment 20 feet square was dedicated to 2,000 skulls kept behind glass, including 'a great number of European, Tartar, Chinese, Maori, Negro and Hottentot skulls, and also examples of the South American races'.[40] One chamber housed hand and foot bones, while another contained larger disconnected dry bones: femurs, hip bones, back bones, shoulder bones. 'And,' added another visiting scientist, 'a number of heads of savages, covered in their own desiccated and tattooed skin'.[41] This was where Saartjie's unburied remains were kept under lock and key, protected 'from the hands of any but privileged visitors'.[42] It was from here, and from collections like this one, that the pseudo-sciences of ethnography and scientific racism were invented in order to propose theories about human racial difference.

After his dinner, Cuvier would take his notebook and wood-burning stove[43] into his gallery of natural classification, where he worked deep into the night, trying to penetrate the recesses of nature, looking for the patterns that he believed would reveal the deepest mysteries of creation[44] encoded in African female sexuality. His brother Frédéric, who was in charge of the zoo, disturbed by Cuvier's pathological obsessions, described him privately as 'master of the charnel house'.[45]

Linnaeus and Buffon had described the exteriors of both living and fossil forms; Cuvier studied the interiors.[46] Comparing fossils with living species, dissecting molluscs and animals, he was the first to base his classifications on comparative anatomy. For earlier zoologists, classification had been based on external resemblances, but Cuvier – anti-Lamarckian, opposed to the notion of a natural hierarchy (*scala naturae*) and anti-evolutionist – argued that without comparative anatomy zoology was worthless. As the founder of palaeontology, he demonstrated that extinct forms were equally as important as living ones in systems of natural classification and used the anatomy of recent animals to aid in the reconstruction of fossil forms.

Cuvier's Cabinet d'Anatomie was not, at this stage, open to the public. Saartjie's body, in life a popular spectacle, became in death a rarefied relic, locked away, viewable, touchable, only by the connoisseur. She became the captive property of science.[47]

At the beginning of 1832, Baron Cuvier was made a peer of France and, shortly before his unexpected death four months later, was appointed Minister of the Interior. Crowds pressed the processional route to Père Lachaise cemetery, where he was honoured with an extravagant state funeral, and a large, reverent entourage attended his burial.[48] No such honour or courtesy had been extended to Saartjie, who did so much to secure Cuvier's fame in the history of science. Her nemesis had left the charnel-house, but her body parts remained immured in the Natural History Museum.

Cuvier's body was also dissected, following his precise instructions. His brain was found to be 'unusually heavy'[49] (1,860 grams) and 'exceptional in the bulging configuration of the lobes'.[50] In a 1908 study that ranked the capacities of 115 'men of note'[51] by brain weight, Turgenev's came first, Cuvier's third. Women's brains were excluded from the study.[52]

One and a half centuries later, the bell-jar containing Saartjie's preserved genitals was rediscovered stored alongside the brains of illustrious nineteenth-century scientists, 'all white and all male',[53] including Cuvier's. The palaeontolgist Stephen Jay Gould, in search of the preserved brain of the famous anatomist, anthropologist and neurologist Paul Broca, happened upon three jars, labelled *une négresse, une péruvienne, and la Vénus Hottentote*.[54]

In the ideological machinery of racist imperialism, Cuvier represented the controlling power of the transcendent, rational, white, intellectual masculine mind over the irrational, excessive, carnal embodiment of Saartjie's dark feminine matter. However, in the battle for mind over matter, the legacy of Saartjie's flesh would prevail. Anglo-French science and culture consigned The Hottentot Venus to gross corporeality and in so doing conjured an unquiet spectral body that, nearly two centuries later, returned to haunt them and demand justice.

Saartjie's bottom became one of the most famous objects of the nineteenth century. Yet, unlike her brain, it was preserved not as physical matter but as legend, popular myth, caricature and racist stereotype. Drawing on the mytheme of The Hottentot Venus, Charles Darwin and Henry Havelock Ellis preoccupied themselves with the racial and sexual signification of black buttocks. Darwin typified the generally held European view that the bottoms of so-called 'Hottentot' women provided a 'somewhat comic sign of the primitive, grotesque nature of black female sexuality'.[55] French and British pornographers shared this fascination and profited from its exploitation.

From successive dissection and analysis of Saartjie's remains, Western European science and philosophy traduced improbable and degrading theories about the buttocks of Khoisan women. These disciplines attempted to dignify and justify their prejudice by claiming that big bottoms were not simply natural physiology but a medical condition they categorised as 'steatopygia'. For all its putative objectivity, there was evidently an underlying agenda: the pursuit of fantasies about primitive and unconstrained − thus 'uncivilised' − female sexual appetites, which both fascinated and appalled masculine intellectual élites.

In 1850 Charles Darwin's cousin Francis Galton, who coined the term *eugenics*, visited what is today Namibia, where he was fascinated to meet a 'Venus among Hottentots' endowed with 'that gift of bounteous nature to this favoured race, which no mantua-maker, with all her crinoline and stuffing, can do otherwise than humbly imitate'.[56] Galton

'boldly pulled out' his measuring-tape and sextant[57] to evaluate the privy parts and nether regions of a woman he
likened to the legendary Saartjie. Galton's bottom-measuring
'experiment' made a telling remark in its aside about the
contemporary fashion for the artificially built-up bottom.
Later in the nineteenth century, the streets of London, the
boulevards of Paris and the thoroughfares of Cape Town
through which she had walked were teeming with women got
up in synthetically constructed fashion steatopygia, vaunted
as the height of civilised European style. What the English
mincingly referred to as the tournure dress improver, or
bustle, the French called simply *le faux-cul* – false bum.

In Galton's time, whalebone, crinoline and stuffing were
the only options available for simulating a large bottom.
Galton would hardly have anticipated that two centuries
later surgeons would be redrawing the outlines of the
female *gluteus maximus* not with measuring-tape and sextant
but with scalpels and silicone implants. At the beginning of
the twenty-first century, buttock augmentation surgery
became the fastest-growing cosmetic procedure in America
and Europe. In Britain, the demand for the 'plump rump'
increased tenfold, while across the Atlantic there was a five-
fold increase.[58] This procedure involves implanting bags of
silicone or quantities of fat removed from elsewhere in the
body into the buttocks, thus making them more pronounced.
Ninety per cent of people who have this surgery are female.
Patients report the pain to be excruciating but are delighted
and amazed by the end results. Surgeons describe themselves as tasked with creating a balance between curviness
and sexiness, 'like a Renaissance painting'.[59]

Could the great men of nineteenth-century science who

had so much to say on the subject of Saartjie's bottom – Cuvier, De Blainville, Darwin and Havelock Ellis – have imagined that centuries later their professional descendents would be performing consensual surgery on women with gluteal deficiencies in order to recreate them in the image of The Hottentot Venus?

How Saartjie would have laughed.[60]

11

LAYING DOWN THE BONES

It took Saartjie three months to get to Europe and two centuries to get back home to South Africa.

At an unknown date between 1822 and the 1850s,[1] the keepers of the Museum of Natural History in Paris placed her skeleton, body-cast, brain and genitals on public display; and there they remained for over a century. The South African paleoanthropologist Professor Phillip Tobias, a life-long champion of South Africa's right to have Saartjie's remains returned, saw them on public display in 1955.[2] In the 1970s the bottled specimens disappeared into storage, and in 1976 the skeleton and body-cast were removed from open exhibition.[3] It was four years later that Saartjie's brain and genitalia were accidentally rediscovered by Stephen Jay Gould in the museum's storerooms.[4]

Fittingly, the end of apartheid in South Africa was the crucial turning-point in Saartjie's afterlife. In 1994, the year the African National Congress achieved the country's tran-sition to non-racial democracy, then President Nelson Mandela raised the matter of Saartjie directly with the

French President François Mitterrand during his first state visit to South Africa. In formally claiming right of possession to Saartjie's remains, Mandela declared the new state's commitment to honouring her as a heroic ancestor and committed the first international act of reclaiming cultural property on behalf of the people of free South Africa. Saartjie became part of the process of transformation from the very moment of liberation.

In 1995 Ben Ngubane, Minister of Arts, Culture, Science and Technology, announced the government's commitment to have Saartjie's remains returned for proper and dignified burial in the land of her birth. 'Our view within government,' Ngubane said,

> has always been that, as she was a known-in-life person and a symbol of an era of oppression and colonialism, her remains should be repatriated to South Africa, without any imputation that either England or France, the French Government, the French people or scholars are to be blamed for the parlous treatment which she received in Europe between 1810 and 1815.[5]

Professor Tobias was appointed to lead the negotiations with the French authorities. His chief negotiating partner was the museologist Henry de Lumley, then director of the Musée de l'Homme and Natural History Museum in Paris, and therefore the official custodian of Saartie's remains.

Saartjie quickly became a potent symbol for political and cultural restitution. The National Khoisan Consultative Conference, led by Cecil Le Fleur, who lobbied for international recognition of the Khoisan as indigenous first peoples, also pressed the French government to send back her relics.[6] In their view, Saartjie represented the suffering of all Khoisan people. Women's-rights activists, poets, artists, academics and politicians raised their voices on her behalf. In August 1998, the United Nations Working Group on Indigenous Populations accorded first-nation status to the Khoisan, strengthening the call for Saartjie's return.

From the outset of the protracted negotiations, South Africa made it clear to France that it regarded Saartjie's case as unique, not as the forerunner to similar requests for the repatriation of thousands of skulls, skeletons and cultural objects in museums in Europe, North America and Australasia, which had been removed during colonial times, mostly without the informed consent of their rightful owners.[7] Saartjie was a special case, famous in her lifetime and after, who had become, in Professor Tobias's words, an 'international symbol of colonial and imperial excesses'.[8] At the national level, another argument supported the claim; there were many Baartmans living in South Africa who might share Saartjie's lineage.[9]

The French museums proved initially resistant, anxious that Saartjie's release would create a flood of further requests from post-colonial nation-states for the return of artifacts plundered by imperial adventurers, thus stripping Western museums. At first, De Lumley resisted, arrogantly claiming that Saartjie's relics would be safer 'cherished in the home of liberty, fraternity and equality, than in South Africa'.[10] Brigitte Mabandla, Deputy Minister of Arts, Culture, Science and Technology, challenged this intransigence:

The end of colonialism is tied to the return of Africa's cultural heritage: Europe doesn't understand the passion of many colonized peoples to right the wrongs of the past. Scholars argue that two hundred year old remains should be classified as ordinary artifacts, and tools for research, and that there is no need to attach emotions to them. This is a fallacy. Europe is littered with ancient heritage, and there is a lot of passion associated with heritage by the Europeans themselves. Humankind remains attached to what is valuable and cultural. Saartjie Baartman's remains are very meaningful to a large majority of South Africans.[11]

During the negotiations, the whereabouts of Saartjie's viscera became unclear. De Lumley, in contradiction to his earlier admission of their existence, suddenly claimed that they had been destroyed in the early 1980s when the shelf on which they were stored had collapsed. However, in 2002 the museum suddenly relocated them. This led to later suggestions that the organs returned to South Africa might not in fact be Saartjie's.[12]

Classified as part of French national patrimony, Saartjie's remains could not leave the country permanently unless allowed to by a change in the law. By October 2000, the dialogue between Tobias and De Lumley had reached an impasse. In November, Ben Ngubane interceded, supported by President Thabo Mbeki, and broke the deadlock. The highly publicised return of the nameless 'El Negro' to Botswana augmented the legitimacy of South Africa's request for Saartjie. El Negro was a southern African warrior whose corpse had been grave-robbed in the early nineteenth century by two respected French naturalists. His stuffed body and personal effects finally ended up in a museum in the small Spanish town of Bagnoles. Following a decade of protest and diplomacy, Spain agreed to return him to Botswana in 2000.[13]

Saartjie also had political allies in France who ardently supported South Africa's claim for her return, in particular the Research Minister Roger-Gerard Schwartzenberg and Senator Nicolas About, who set about framing legislation to permit the repatriation of her remains. A report by the French Senate demonstrated that a rift had opened up on the issue between the state and the guardians of culture. The report criticised the museums for 'incompetence fighting with absurdity'[14] and, with a perhaps unwitting pun, accused them of 'grave management dysfunction'.[15]

Finally, on 29 January 2002, the French Senate voted to release Saartjie's remains from the Musée de l'Homme. Speaking in the Senate, Schwartzenberg said that her return would mark Europe's emergence 'from the long night of slavery, colonialism, and racism',[16] also noting that the law would 'restore full dignity to Saartjie Baartman, who was humiliated as a woman and exploited as an African'.[17] About made a passionate address: 'This young woman was treated as if she was something monstrous. But where in this affair is the true monstrosity?'[18] He also read out 'I Have Come to Take You Home – a Tribute to Saartjie Baartman' by the South African poet Diana Ferrus, who is of Khoisan descent:

> I have come to wrench you away –
> away from the poking eyes
> of the man-made monster

who lives in the dark
with his clutches of imperialism
who dissects your body bit by bit
who likens your soul to that of Satan
and declares himself the ultimate god![19]

Ferrus's poem was highly influential in persuading the French Senate to support the bill giving Saartjie a human face and personalising her plight. The legislation went to the National Assembly for approval, and on 21 February it voted unanimously for Saartjie's return to South Africa.

On 29 April, a week before Jacques Chirac went to the polls to face the anti-immigrant Jean-Marie Le Pen in the election battle of 5 May, the French government formally handed over Saartjie's remains in a ceremony held at the South African Embassy in Paris. Thuthukile Skweyiya, the South African ambassador to France, announced, 'Saartjie Baartman is beginning her final journey home, to a free, democratic, non-sexist and non-racist South Africa. She is a symbol of our national need to confront our past and restore dignity to all our people.'[20]

Specialised packagers of human remains carefully arranged Saartjie's diminutive skeleton, pearl-white and luminous, in a foam-lined box. The two glass bell-jars and the full-body plaster cast were also crated and returned. Painted brown and gaudily varnished, the synthetic surface of the cast contrasted oddly with its life-like form. Foam packaging supported the arms, raised slightly in a gesture of supplication.

On 2 May 2002, South African Airways flight 275 flew through the night from Paris to Johannesburg bearing its historic cargo. The delegation that went to Paris to bring Saartjie home sat among the regular passengers, including Diana Ferrus, whose poem had so inspired the French Senators. For the duration of the flight, Ferrus kept a vigil over Saartjie's remains, stored below in the hold.[21] Just before the plane landed, the captain announced that it was carrying a very special passenger. This time, Saartjie had not travelled in secret.

Saartjie's remains touched South African soil on the bright highveld morning of 3 May 2002. After 187 years, she was home. South Africa greeted her with a rapturous reception, and her repatriation hit the headlines in the national and global media. From Johannesburg, Saartjie's relics were flown to Cape Town International Airport, where once again crowds gathered to welcome her. Her homecoming was set against the backdrop of South Africa's defining landmark: Table Mountain, swathed in its famous tablecloth of cumulous clouds. Shrouded by the new South African flag, her casket was lowered onto the runway to the accompaniment of a small band of Cape musicians, one of whom played a *ramkie*. Children pressed their faces against the windows of the arrivals terminal. A military band accompanied the official welcoming ceremony, including, elegiacally, a smartly uniformed young drummer.

Saartjie's casket was stored at the morgue of the Wynberg Military Hospital in Cape Town while arrangements were made for her burial. Brigitte Mabandla established a committee to determine the location, date and religious orders for her funeral, and to advise on a fitting monument or commemoration. Initially, Saartjie was to be buried in the Company Gardens in central Cape Town. However, this decision provoked some controversy, so the government undertook a public consultation process to determine her final resting place. After much debate, they decided on Hankey, a small rural town near the banks of the Gamtoos River. The rocky mount (*koppie*) chosen for her grave is called Vergaderingskop, meaning 'meeting hill'. Vergaderingskop overlooks the emerald-green and incarnadine earth of the Gamtoos River Valley, encircled by indigo mountains and sheltered by a sky that, in the words of the Langston Hughes poem read by President Mbeki at Saartjie's burial, turns 'all golden in the sunset'.[22] The funeral was set for 9 August, Women's Day in South Africa and international Indigenous Peoples' Day.

On Sunday, 4 August, a Khoisan cleansing ritual and dressing ceremony took place at the Cape Town civic theatre, to prepare Saartjie for burial. Brigitte Mabandla explained that the ritual was meant to celebrate Saartjie's memory 'through poetry, song and by providing a platform for all South Africans to express solidarity in her memory'.[23] The ceremony combined tradition and modern invention.

Saartjie's return became a rallying point for the descendents of Khoisan people in search of their ancestral identity. The funeral preparations caused some discord among those who felt excluded from the consultation process, such as the The Korana First Nation of South Africa, who felt that politicians had hijacked her homecoming. Some families claimed to be Saartjie's direct descendants. Khoisan historian Nealroy Swarts questioned the reliability of these assertions but welcomed the debate: 'It is good to know that people are starting to make claims of their heritage. That is something we must be proud of. This is our grandmother. This is the nation's grandmother.'[24]

Baartman is a very common South African surname; there are Baartmans among all races and religions. While there is currently no firm evidence confirming Saartjie's immediate descendents, academics continue to research her lineage and perhaps may solve the question.[25] Saartjie became a powerful symbol of integration and inclusion for all of South Africa's formerly divided racial groups. As Willa Boezak put it, '[When] we celebrate her homecoming it will be a spiritual ceremony. It will be a reburial. It will not be a Cape Town thing, it will not be a Griqua[26] thing, it will be a national thing.'[27]

Saartjie also became a representative historical figure in South Africa's struggle for gender equality. In Parliament, South African women MPs condemned her exploitation and welcomed the restoration of her dignity.[28] She was honoured by women's-rights activists at rallies and demonstrations.[29] A shelter for women and children subjected to domestic and sexual violence is named after her.[30]

Addressing so many live issues in South Africa, Saartjie became a living ancestor. Nations, like individuals, need myths and icons to salve and heal the psychological and physical injury inflicted by oppressive systems, and inter-nalised over centuries of marginalisation. Saartjie's homecoming was a tangible act to right a historical wrong. The public rituals of mourning and acknowledgement of the injustice she endured provided a means of addressing buried suffering.

About 2,500 people[31] attended Saartjie's state funeral on 9 August 2002. The day was dazzling and fiercely hot. Many handkerchiefs mopped the brows of ministers and dignitaries. Beyond the official enclosures, the throng of celebrants sheltered themselves as best they could from the pitiless sun. It was a day of music, dance, poetry, theatre, praise-singing and speeches. Reporting from the funeral on live national television, Redi Direko summed up the atmosphere:

> Rarely has one figure meant so much to an entire country. In the burial of Saartjie Baartman we have so many issues coming together; the issues of culture, the issues of identity, the issues of cultural reparation after all these years.[32]

Young girls body-hopped, perhaps somewhat incongruously, in scanty bushbuck bikinis. A syncopated diaspora of women of all ages and ethnicities danced together in fine African beadwork, rustling Indian saris and *doeks* (headscarves). The euphonious sounds of friction bows, *gouras* and Saartjie's beloved *ramkie* could be heard all day. Diana Ferrus gave an oration of her now famous poem and proclaimed Saartjie South Africa's great mother and ancestor. Women's leaders, represented by the South African Commission on Gender Equality, said that the greatest tribute South Africa could pay Saartjie was to work for the liberation of women from sexual slavery, violence, abuse, poverty and disease.

Speakers at the funeral emphasised that Saartjie's homecoming empowered Africans to reclaim personal dignity and helped the continent to overcome its marginalisation.

Nealroy Swarts reminded the mourners that European colonisation had decimated Khoisan culture and society: there were approximately twenty-two Khoisan tribes at the Cape when Jan van Riebeeck arrived in 1652; now there are only two. Ben Ngubane commemorated Saartjie's ancestors and descendents: '. . . they were all victims of a vicious system, a system that could declare a people, a land, a culture, to be subservient to a distant monarch somewhere in Europe.'[33] Brigitte Mabandla described how, when visiting schools, she found that every child knew about Saartjie. Her life, the Deputy Minister said, should be taught as part of the school history curriculum, as an example for the rejection of racist historical iconography. Saartjie's story, Mabandla concluded, offered 'an education for the public in our own past'.[34]

The remembrance and revision of racist history, and the legacy of European science, were the central themes of President Mbeki's speech. Challenging those who 'urge constantly that we should not speak of the past',[35] Mbeki illustrated how Saartjie was exploited by leading European scientists to prove their xenophobic theories about white superiority. He detailed the racist observations to be found in the philosophising of the luminaries of the Enlightenment such as Voltaire, Montesquieu and Diderot. Juxtaposing notions of European civilisation with historical assumptions about African barbarism, Mbeki reversed this logic to demonstrate the barbarism of ostensibly civilised European culture. He cited damning passages from Cuvier's report on Saartjie's dissection.[36] On hearing these gruesomely pornographic, bigoted descriptions spoken by the president, several youngsters in the audience wept and fainted. Their visceral reactions exemplified the problems associated with the requirement to reproduce racist representation in order to expose it to criticism.[37]

Commending the contemporary French politicians who, by supporting Saartjie's rightful repatriation, challenged the legacy of European barbarism and global imperialism, Mbeki said that by so doing they finally lived up to the noble objectives of liberty, equality and fraternity. Apartheid, he reminded his audience, was also 'based on the criminal notion that some had been called upon to enlighten the hordes of barbarians, as Sarah Bartmann was enlightened and tamed'.

The president congratulated all women on National Women's Day, marking South Africa's responsibility to move speedily towards the creation of a non-sexist society. Women, Mbeki said, had borne the brunt of oppression and exploitation under colonial and apartheid domination: 'They, more than the African male, were presented as the very representation of what was savage and barbaric about all our people.' Even now, he reminded his audience, women in South Africa continue to carry the burden of poverty, unacceptable violence and abuse.

Mbeki stressed that the nation identified with the burden of Saartjie's pain and intolerable misery: 'When we turn away from this grave of a simple African woman, a particle of each one of us will stay with the remains of Sarah Bartmann.' Intended to be respectful, this reference to Saartjie as a simple African woman struck an odd, patronising note. Mbeki's speech clearly accounted for the ways in which Saartjie was sexually and racially subjugated as an object of pornographic representation, but failed to comment on the exploitation of her physical labour, either as a domestic servant or as a 'carnal curiosity'.[38]

Mbeki's speech at Saartjie's funeral focussed on the role of medical history in the sexual ideology of colonial and apartheid racism. His critical analysis of the nineteenth-century European scientists and philosophers who abused the body of Saartjie Baartman was accurate, but the manner in which he yoked this history to an attempt to justify his own public health policies was not. As is well known, President Mbeki controversially denies the causal link between the HIV virus and AIDS, a position that has come to be known as a policy of denialism. Mbeki also supports claims that anti-retroviral drugs are ineffective and lethally toxic, in the face of massive scientific evidence to the contrary, and in contradiction of the experience of people living with HIV who have access to ARV treatment.

In July 2000, at the 13th International AIDS Conference in Durban, South Africa, 5,000 researchers and scientists from around the world issued the 'Durban Declaration' to challenge Mbeki, affirming that HIV causes AIDS, a statement that his press secretary declared as fit only for the 'dustbin'. Mbeki's reluctance to make AIDS drugs available, and his perceived support for the right-wing American AIDS 'dissidents', led critics from within South Africa and the rest of the world to charge Mbeki with 'irresponsibility bordering on criminality',[39] and to call the South African government's official position on AIDS genocidal.

In 2000, Mbeki appointed two controversial American AIDS 'dissidents' – who defy mainstream opinion that AIDS is caused by the HIV virus – to a presidential advisory board on the epidemic. Nelson Mandela publicly rebuked Mbeki for his stance on AIDS in South Africa. Thus the focus of this speech at Saartjie's funeral was significant. When Thabo Mbeki talks *publicly* about European science and its relation to Africa, the message is clear: he is engaging on the troubled battleground of HIV/AIDS. Allusions to the pandemic haunted his entire funeral address, and this speech is seen as a rare statement on a subject he rarely speaks about in public.[40]

As Mbeki stood at Saartjie's graveside, his government was engaged in a fierce court battle to prevent HIV-positive women from accessing Nevirapine, a drug endorsed by the World Health Organisation that limits mother-to-child transmission (MTCT) and thus saves the lives of children. In 1994 it was established that treatment with the antiretroviral drug AZT dramatically reduces the risk of MTCT transmission. Despite Mbeki's statement that 'It will never be possible for us to claim that we are making significant progress to create a new South Africa if we do not make significant progress towards gender equality and the emancipation of women,' as he spoke his government ignored the raised voices of hundreds of thousands of women demanding the right to such life-saving drug treatments.[41]

On the crest of Vergaderingskop, the burial ceremony began with the burning of *buchu*, a sweet-smelling medicinal herb, to purify Saartjie's spirit. Khoisan chiefs broke a bow and arrows and scattered them into the grave in traditional observance of the ancestors. As a women's choir sang softly in the background, 'You are returning to your fatherland under African skies', Saartjie's coffin, decorated with aloe wreaths, was lowered into the ground.

12

AFTERLIFE

Saartjie died in 1815 and was buried in 2002. Her bones never gathered dust. For two centuries, The Hottentot Venus appeared in European science, art, literature, philosophy and popular culture, choreographed to the macabre dance of racial and sexual prejudice. European racism made Saartjie a Frankenstein's monster of its own invention. Subdued and dismembered, Saartjie's relics became the haunting agent of her posthumous retribution. Through them, western imperialism would be called to account for its inhumanity.

Andreas Vesalius, the father of anatomical dissection, believed that 'the violation of the body would be the revelation of its truth.'[1] Imprisoned in the Natural History Museum in Paris, Saartjie's disarticulated body became one of Europe's most frequently analysed specimens, and many of the biographical truths of her existence disappeared beneath the burden of her afterlife as an object of science.

For two hundred years, Saartjie's skeleton was rattled, her dead brain dissected, her genital matter fingered by inquisitive European men who believed that her pickled organs held secrets that would reveal the mysteries of the 'dark continent'[2] of African female sexuality. From these lifeless and fragile remnants of Saartjie's violated body, scientists manufactured monstrous, crackpot theories proposing biological racial differences between human groups. There was, they argued, more than one species in the genus *Homo*; races could be classified, and ranked in terms of superiority and inferiority. The motivation was obvious: the desire to justify inequalities of power.

De Blainville (1816) and Cuvier (1817) superimposed the template of scientific racism upon Saartjie's remains. Scientists, ethnographers, anthropologists, philosophers and psychologists followed them. In the period of scientific racism and eugenics, her dismembered body was used as the ultimate example to propound the belief that races existed and were biologically different. According to these pseudo sciences, Europeans were at the top of the human scale of evolution in the Great Chain of Being, Africans at the bottom; and the so-called 'Hottentots' and 'Bushmen' of sub-Saharan Africa were the missing link to the animal species. Allegedly degenerate and brutally inferior, 'Hottentots' were assigned the 'lowest' rank among the admissibly human.[3] British imperialism incorporated this specious science into its ruling ideology in South Africa. The apartheid regime followed suit.

Aided and abetted by Charles Darwin and the Comte de Gobineau, the implications of the discovery of geneties in the nineteenth century was abused and distorted in order to provide a supposedly scientific justification to racism. In the nineteenth century, Saartjie was the ultimate example used to 'prove' the existence of biological racial difference and eugenics. From the holocaust to apartheid, these theories were used to justify the worst atrocities and injustices of the twentieth century.

Although Saartjie lived only a short life, her remains finally outlived the lie of inherent racial difference. The discovery of DNA in the 1950s proved that race is a socially constructed phenomenon with no biological basis, thus consigning scientific racism and eugenics to the dustbin of history. Found in the nucleus of cells, the DNA molecule determines human physical characteristics by providing the set of instructions from which the body is built: 'There are no inferior races: there are no races; there is practically no racial differentiation among humans.'[4] In 1950 and '52, UNESCO's international meetings of scientists declared that race was a social myth, not a biological fact, and that humans belong to the single species *Homo sapiens*, and recommended dropping the term *race* altogether. Visual differences 'in physical structure which distinguish one major group from another [were judged to] give no support to the popular notions of any general "superiority" or "inferiority" which are sometimes implied in referring to . . . groups.'[5] Scientists told the world that the facts of biology had made racism indefensible and that humans are one and the same group: 'The likenesses among men are far greater than their differences.'[6]

Thus science finally conceded that the visual differences between humans are meaningless. However, the disproving of scientific theories, even when they are publicly revoked, does not have the power to reverse or erase the psychic and cultural impact of the legacy of race and racism, as the example of Saartjie's life demonstrates.[7]

Some expressed the hope that Saartjie's burial would lay her spirit to rest. But traumatic memory is not easily buried. As Sylvia Vollenhoven expressed it on South African television on the day of her funeral, 'Sarah Baartman is no longer Sarah Baartman. She has become a symbol for the women of our country.'[8] A symbol of the alienation and degradations of colonisation, lost children, exile, the expropriation of female labour, and the sexual and economic exploitation of black women by men, white and black, Saartjie has come to represent the pain and suffering of all exploited black women, and the psychic, cultural and emotional impact of racism and its legacy. This was what Thabo Mbeki stressed in his graveside representation of Saartjie, casting her as a passive victim subject entirely to the will of others. She had been used, he reminded her mourners, to prove

> . . . the alleged promiscuity of the African women who, it was claimed, invited either man or ape . . . Sarah Baartman was taken to Europe to tell this lie in the most dramatic way possible. She was ferried to Europe as an example of the sexual depravity and the incapacity to think of the African woman in the first instance and the African in general. The legacy of those centuries remains with us, both in the way in which our society is structured and in the ideas that many in our country continue to carry in their heads, which inform their reaction on important matters.[9]

However, as with all sanctified women, the archetype of the silenced victim threatens to engulf Saartjie's individualism and humanity. Toni Morrison has written critically of how, in the conventions of racist storytelling, a black woman is '[r]endered voiceless, a cipher, a perfect victim'.[10] Saartjie suffered, but she endured and, as far as she could, rebelled. As an orphan, as a woman, as a curious, adventurous individual, she stepped always on the edge of danger, surviving for as long as possible in extraordinarily challenging circumstances.

Throughout her life Saartjie had to suffer for her race as well; her experience might prompt an instinctive loyalty to the notion of race and sexuality as the defining factors in her life, yet this notion leaves her unfree. It is part of women's historical burden to be made representative, and this is the danger of memorialising Saartjie as a passive victim. As she realised throughout her life, being placed on a pedestal as an object of degradation, veneration or both is potentially fatal – and opposable. Sanctification never set a woman's spirit free. The dangers of not looking for the acts of resistance in Saartjie's life, however small they may seem now, are greater than those of sentimentalising her story. As long as Saartjie is seen as inescapably constrained by her race and gender, history will still have its foot on her neck.

Saartjie, who lost her father as an infant, has ever since been fought over by patriarchs. In life and after, she was and has been a constant preoccupation for men, from soldiers, sailors, doctors and traders to scientists, politicians and philosophers, many of whom were among the most prominent men of their age. Some were progressive; most were not.

South Africa's first two democratic presidents took direct responsibility for Saartjie's legacy, intervening personally to determine its outcome. By asking France to return Saartjie, Nelson Mandela announced to the world that South Africa could forgive but not forget and that Europe needed to make active reparation for the past. Thabo Mbeki took over the baton and supported her return; he also brought Saartjie into the frontline of some of the most vexed issues of modern South Africa: his vision of the African Renaissance, the HIV/AIDS crisis, and the legacy of racism.

Thabo Mbeki has consistently questioned the evidence-based, scientifically proven causal link between HIV and AIDS, and has made it clear that his sympathies lie with propagators of AIDS denialism. The consequence: huge delays in the roll-out of antiretroviral (ARV) treatment programmes in the public health sector, resulting in, to date, an estimated 75,000 avoidable deaths.

Despite this AIDS denialism from the presidency and Health Minister Manto Tshabalala-Msimang, the broadening of democracy in South Africa has created space for civil society organisations to campaign for equitable access to affordable treatment. In 2006, in response to the sustained national mobilisation of the Treatment Action Campaign and its advocacy of global support for fighting the HIV/AIDS epidemic, some progress has been made towards the South African government's commitment to delivering a national strategic plan to promote and provide adequate ARV medicines and treatment for people with HIV.

Saartjie's resting-place has not been left in peace. Even on the day of her funeral, rumours sprang up around her grave. A local policeman claimed that the remains buried at Hankey were not hers. According to this canard, the government retained her relics in an undisclosed location because of the risk of extortion: villains might dig them up and hold them to ransom. Saartjie's funeral was the biggest event ever to take place in Hankey, a region racked by underinvestment and endemic economic deprivation; her body remained an object on which to attach speculative economic value.

In September 2003, the decomposing body of a four-year-old boy was discovered shallowly buried beneath a bush by her grave.[11] In March 2005, vandals removed the memorial nameplate from a rock near her burial place, provoking an angry response from the government. But even as conspiracy, child murder and desecration were troubling Saartjie's resting-place, she was being memorialised elsewhere as a pre-eminent figure in South Africa's ancestral, political and cultural heritage. In January 2005, the government took delivery of the *Sarah Baartman*, a state-of-the-art offshore environmental-protection vessel made in Holland.[12]

Saartjie continues to be a venerated and contested figure in South Africa. The return of her remains has also made her a global icon, as recognised in the annals of British and French history as she is in the townships and schools of South Africa. Founded upon the principle of non-racial democracy, with probably the most progressive democratic constitution in the world, South Africa chose Saartjie as an important ancestor to symbolise the restoration of the dignity and humanity of all of its peoples. Controversy and debate will continue to haunt her troubled life and legacy, but it is now possible to say that Saartjie Baartman has truly come home.

NOTES

1 PHOENOMENON

[1] Georges Cuvier, *Report on Observations Made on the Body of a Woman Known in Paris and in London as the Hottentot Venus*, Memoires du Muséum d'Histoire Naturelle (Paris: 1817).

[2] This and all proceeding citations from this episode are from Anne Mathews, *Memoirs of Charles Mathews, Comedian*, vol. IV (London, 1839), pp. 133–7.

[3] As well as an actor, Kemble was an innovative manager. In 1788 he introduced live animals to the London stage for the first time.

[4] Originating from Africa and the Indian subcontinent, 'Baba' is now a common form of address across the world. In languages with Nguni roots, as spoken by Saartjie, 'Baba' is the term of respect reserved for fathers, elders and men of a certain age and status. Khoisan shares a common root with Xhosa and Zulu. In Xhosa, 'utata' means 'father'. It is notable that Kemble, an actor known for his deliberate enunciation, correctly interprets this term that Mathews finds 'unintelligible'. In Hindi, which also influenced sub-Saharan African languages, 'Baba' is a term of endearment. It means 'father' or 'grandfather', but in common usage may be applied to people of any age about whom one feels particular affection and respect.

⁵ Anna H. Smith, 'Still More about the Hottentot Venus', *Africana Notes and News*, 26/3 (September 1984), Africana Society, Africana Museum, City of Johannesburg.

⁶ *Morning Herald*, 20 September 1810, p. 1.

2 *M TAI !NUERRE* – 'MY MOTHER'S COUNTRY'

¹ This /Xam phrase, meaning home, is from a well known San folk-story called 'The Moon and the Hare'. See Janette Deacon and Thomas Dowson (eds.) *Voices from the Past: /Xam Bushmen and the Bleek and Lloyd Collection* (Johannesburg: Witwatersrand University Press, 1996)

² 'Examination of the Hottentot Venus', 27 November 1810, affidavit, KB1/36, pt IV, King's Bench, Court Records, The National Archives (TNA, formerly Public Record Office), London.

³ All of the big five inhabited the region: elephant, rhino, leopard, lion and buffalo.

⁴ Common name for the genus euphorbia.

⁵ Despite strenuous arguments to the contrary by nineteenth-century ethnographers, anthropological evidence clearly shows that the Khoekhoen and the San emerged from one people and were not separate races. The Khoekhoen became a distinct class in the late Stone Age, when their society shifted from hunting and gathering to animal husbandry and pastoralism. While the Khoekhoen became farmers, the San retained their seasonally shifting bush-culture. Over time, the San, whose livelihood was more precarious, were employed as servants, hunters and soldiers by the cattle-rich Khoekhoen. The collective term *Khoisan* (*Khoi* or *Khoe*, and *San*) is now used when speaking of the long shared history of South Africa's first peoples, to explicitly reject both antiquated colonial notions about 'Bushmen' and 'Hottentots' and the freight of racism inextricable from the etymology of these terms. See Shula Marks, 'Khoisan Resistance to the Dutch in the

Seventeenth and Eighteenth Centuries', *Journal of African History*, 13/1 (1972), pp. 55–80, esp. p. 57.

[6] See Richard Dawkins, 'Ecology of Genes', in *A Devil's Chaplin: Selected Essays* (London, 2004), p. 265.

[7] While it is possible that the family retained Khoisan names, 'Baartman' was clearly passed to Saartjie by her father. There are three possibilities regarding the provenance of the name. First, from the 1650s the children of marriages between colonists and local women or slaves inherited the names of their white fathers. Second, it was common practice for masters/employers to impose their patronymics onto employees whose names they could not pronounce. But we know the name of Saartjie's first employees, and it was not Baartman, so the name clearly predates her first employment. Third, masters/employees would foist made-up names onto their employees as a form of subjugation. The literal meaning of 'Baartman' is 'bearded man'. It carries the archaic sense in which beardedness is a respected mark of masculinity, indicating adult manliness. It can equally simply be taken to describe an extremely hairy man.

[8] For a more detailed account of the Khoisan language, see Megan Biesele, 'Stories and Storage: Transmission of Ju/' Hoan Knowledges and Skills', paper presented at the 9th International Conference on Hunting and Gathering Societies, Edinburgh, 9–13 September 2002.

[9] In reality, the divisions were arbitrary; a Khoekhoen without cattle who reverted to hunting and gathering became a Bushman, while a Bushman who worked for white settlers was seen as Khoekhoen.

[10] See Marks, 'Khoisan Resistance' pp. 55–80, esp. p. 55. These stereotypes have been extensively documented in academic work on this history of negative representation. See, for example, Linda Schiebinger, *Nature's Body: Gender in the Making of Modern Science* (Boston, 1993); Z. S. Strother, 'Display of the Body Hottentot', in Bernth Lindfors, ed., *Africans on Stage: Studies in Ethnological Show Business* (Bloomington and Indianapolis, 1999), pp. 1–61.

[11] *Hottentot* was the term by which Saartjie came to be defined, but she was also frequently described as a 'Bushman' and sometimes,

by Europeans scholars perplexed by their own inventions, a 'Bushman-Hottentot'. These terms were in common usage in her childhood and were part of her own vocabulary. Conversing in Afrikaans, she used the Dutch-Afrikaans variant of *Bosmen* (also *Bosjesman*) to describe the San people she knew from that time. For example, see 'Examination of the Hottentot Venus', 27 November 1810, pt IV.

[12] In ancient times, the Xhosa spearheaded the expansion of the Nguni peoples into the African subcontinent, a migration that originated in the Cameroon. The Xhosa and the Zulu, also part of this movement, were the two key groups who settled in what is now known as South Africa. Archaeological research suggests that the earliest presence of Nguni Iron-Age pastoralists in south-eastern Africa can be dated to around the seventh and eighth centuries. Xhosa polity and society were structured around vast cattle herds, strict codes of hospitality, a disposition to peace and negotiation rather than war, and fierce loyalty to their chiefs, who led democratic decision-making and judicial processes. The principal cultural characteristics of the Xhosa suggest Semitic origins and, many believe, are derived from Mosaic law. Over centuries, the Xhosa-speaking nations diversified into many interrelated chiefdoms and peoples, structured around the key divisions into Pondo, Tembu and Xhosa. The Xhosa settled in the area now known as the Eastern Cape and emerged into a number of clans, chief among them being the Gcaleka, Ngika, Ndlambe, Dushane, Qayi, Ntinde and, of Khoisan origin, the Gqunkhwebe. Between 1670 and 1770 two major schisms occurred in Xhosa society. These splits, and the resulting authority crisis, was the cause of the westward migration towards the Fish River by breakaway chiefdoms. See Noël Mostert, *Frontiers: The Epic of South Africa's Creation and the Tragedy of the Xhosa People* (London, 1992); Hermann Gilomee, 'The Eastern Frontier, 1770–1812', in Richard Elphick and Hermann Gilomee, eds, *The Shaping of South African Society: 1652–1820* (Cape Town, 1979), pp. 291–337; Ben

Maclennan, *A Proper Degree of Terror: John Graham and the Cape's Eastern Frontier* (Johannesburg, 1986).

[13] Giliomee, 'The Eastern Frontier', pp. 291–337, esp. p. 297.

[14] Travellers and, later, anthropologists claimed that this instrument was played only by Khoisan men.

[15] Marks, 'Khoisan Resistance', pp. 55–80, esp. p. 78. In a crowded field, Professor Marks's account remains one of the clearest and most accurate expositions.

[16] For this account of Khoekhoen employment on the eastern frontier, see Richard Elphick, 'The Khoisan to c. 1770', in Elphick and Giliomee, eds, *The Shaping of South African Society*, pp. 3–33, esp. p. 27.

[17] 'Examination of the Hottentot Venus', pt IV.

[18] Marks, 'Khoisan Resistance' p. 73.

[19] Nigel Penn, 'The Frontier in the Western Cape', in John Parkington and Martin Hall, eds, *Papers in the Prehistory of the Western Cape*, BAR International Series 332 (Oxford, 1987), Robert Shell, *Children of Bondage: A Social History of the Slave Society at the Cape of Good Hope, 1652–1838* (Johannesburg 1994), pp. 30–32.

[20] *Report from the Select Committee on Aborigines* (British Settlements) with the Minutes of Evidence, Appendix and Index, London, House of Commons, 26 June 1837, p. 28, cited in Shell, *Children of Bondage*, p. 32.

[21] See Caitlin Davies, *The Return of El Negro: The Compelling Story of Africa's Unknown Soldier* (London, 2003), p. 13.

[22] Marks, 'Khoisan Resistance', p. 75.

[23] See 'Examination of the Hottentot Venus', pt IV; and *Inventoris Van Opgaafrolle, Kaapstad en Kaapse Distrik, Opgaafrolle* 1/5, (1807), Government Archives, Cape Town, J41, p. 70.

[24] 'La Vénus hottentote', *Journal des dames et des modes*, 25 January 1815, pp. 37–40.

[25] The cattle runs divided between legal trade with the Dutch East India Company and illegal trade with *trekboers* and settler farmers.

[26] Marks, 'Khoisan Resistance', p. 67; Mostert, *Frontiers*; Gilomee,

'The Eastern Frontier', pp. 291–337; Ben Maclennan, *A Proper Degree of Terror*.

[27] 'La Vénus hottentote'.

[28] Ibid., p. 37.

[29] Ibid., p. 39.

[30] The guitar, or *ramakib*, was made out of hollowed wood, with a calabash or touch board attached to one end, over which were drawn the strings; the *goura* was a stringed wind instrument common to the Southern Khoisan; and reed flutes are the same everywhere. For an introduction to Khoisan musical instruments, see I. Schapera, *The Khoisan Peoples of South Africa: Bushmen and Hottentots* (London, 1930), pp. 206–7; Deirdre Hansen, 'Bushman Music: Still an Unknown', in Pippa Skotnes, ed., *Miscast: Negotiating the Presence of the Bushmen* (Cape Town, 1996), pp. 297–305.

[31] 'La Vénus hottentote', p. 40.

[32] Ibid., p. 38.

[33] Asked how old she was when she was taken to Cape Town, Saartjie contradicted herself. First she said she was so young that she could not remember, but then she stated categorically that she lived in Cape Town for three years, leaving when she was twenty-one. These factual faultlines reveal something of the distress of her inner life. Trauma may have made her memory evasive and protective, and later she had reason to be cautious and opaque about these events. She also may not have been exactly sure when she was born.

[34] See 'Examination of the Hottentot Venus', pt IV.

3 CITY OF LOST CHILDREN

[1] 'Examination of the Hottentot Venus', 27 November 1810, affidavit, KB1/36, pt IV, King's Bench, Court Records, The National Archives (TNA, formerly Public Record Office), London. Saartjie never specified their mode of travel. The available options were to travel overland or to take a ship from Algoa Bay to Cape Town. As

an itinerant trader, Pieter Cesars was most likely to travel over-land.

[2] Monkey ropes are lianas.

[3] 'La Vénus Hottentote', *Journal des dames et des modes*, 25 January 1815, p. 40.

[4] Philip Edwards, ed., *The Journals of Captain Cook 1768–1779* (London, 1999), p. 205.

[5] *African Court Calendar* (Cape Town, 1810), Government Archives, Cape Town ZI/1/12.

[6] See *Opgaafrolle* 1/5, p. 70.

[7] Reverend John Campbell, London Missionary Society, unpub. sketchbook, Africana Museum, Johannesburg. See Percival Kirby, 'The "Hottentot Venus" of the Musée de l'Homme, Paris', *Suid-Afrikaanse Joernaal van Wetenskap* (July 1954), p. 321.

[8] This Malayan word for 'house' found its way into kitchen-Dutch, then Afrikaans, from the earliest settlement of the Cape. *Pondokkie* is still used in Afrikaans to signify a small, informal, temporary structure.

[9] See the 1807 census, *Opgaafrolle* 1/5, p. 70.

[10] 'Examination of the Hottentot Venus'.

[11] Legislative changes introduced in 1809 made it compulsory to pay Hottentot servants a proper wage.

[12] See Sarah Gertrude Millen, *King of the Bastards* (London, 1950), p. 6.

[13] *Will of Hendrik Cesars en Anna Catharina Staal*, 13 August 1805, MOOC 7/1/61, no. 57 (1811), Government Archives, Cape Town. All citations are from a translation by Robert Symonds and the author.

[14] *Will of Hendrik Cesars en Anna Catharina Staal*. Anna Catharina's parents are recorded as Elisabeth Jacobse and Hendrik Staal, but there is no record of Hendrik and Pieter's parents.

[15] *Will of Hendrik Cesars en Anna Catharina Staal*.

[16] Recorded as 'one daughter under the age of 25' in *Opgaafrolle* 1/5, p. 70.

[17] The Register of Wards of the Orphan Chamber starts in 1825.

There are no known lists of orphans adopted from the Orphan Chamber during the period 1805–8.

[18] See Shell, *Children of Bondage*, pp. 128, 217. There was no orphanage at the Cape to help all children until 1815.

[19] See Shell, *Children of Bondage*, pp. 81–3, 128–30.

[20] See *Opgaafrolle* 1/5, p. 70. On 10 August 1807 the government issued a proclamation ordering a census, to take place until 1 December, covering Cape Town and the surrounding districts. It shows the exact composition of the Cesars' household when Saartjie was working as their nursemaid. The age of the three male 'Hottentot' servants and the two male 'life-slaves' is given as over sixteen. Only the names of the heads of the household were listed; children, 'Hottentot' servants and slaves were simply listed by numbers.

[21] One of these was named January of Mozambique; see 1811 codicil to *Will of Hendrik Cesars en Anna Catharina Staal,* 'our slave boy, January of Mozambique, after we have both died, must be released from the estate – and moreover, a sum of fifty rijks daalders (=125 guilders) shall be paid to him from the estate.'

[22] In what follows, I am indebted to the work of Robert Shell and his team of researchers who have done so much to document and archive the records and literature of slavery at the Cape from its earliest colonisation. Shell in turn draws upon key scholars and pioneers in the field, including (to name but a few) A. J. Böeseken, Shula Marks, Leonard Guelke, Robert Ross, Carmel Schrire, Stanley Trapido and the Elphicks.

[23] A. J. Böeseken, *Slaves and Free Blacks at the Cape 1658–1700* (Cape Town, 1977), p. 5.

[24] See Shell, *Children of Bondage*, p. 42.

[25] Ibid.

[26] Alf Wannenburgh, *Forgotten Frontiersmen* (Lansdowne), p. 22. Also see Böesaken, *Slaves and Free Blacks.* (Cape Town, 1977).

[27] Shell, *Children of Bondage*, p. 374.

[28] This precept of descent over skin colour was carried through into

the hated Population Registration Act of 1950 and allied racial reclassification laws of the apartheid regimes.

[29] Shell, *Children of Bondage*, pp. xxxii–xxxiii.

[30] Hendrik testified that he could not write in his and Anna Catherina's will (*Will of Hendrik Cesars en Anna Catharina Staal*). In the 1810 codicil to the will, the registering clerk recorded, 'This is the mark of the first appearer [Hendrik Cesars] who testified that he could not write.'

[31] See C. C. de Villiers and C. Pama, *Genealogies of South African Families*, vols 1–3; D. F. du Toit Malherbe (Cape Town, 1966), *Family Register of the South African Nation* (Stellenbosch, 1966); R.T.J. Lombard, *Handbook for Genealogical Research in South Africa* (Pretoria, 1977 and 1990); Peter Philip, *British Residents at the Cape: Biographical Records of 4800 Pioneers* (Cape Town, 1981).

[32] See, for examples, '*Caesars van Mosambique*', *Lyst der Transporten van Plaatzen, Slaaven, & mitsgaders Actens van Cesfie gepasfeerd in den jaare 1800*, no. 587 *tot* 748, NCD 1/41, no. 601, 1 Feb 1800; 'Caesar from Batavia', Court of Justice Records, CJ796, no. 42, 1794.

[33] See C. Pama, *Die Groot Afrikaanse Familie-Naamboek* (Johannesburg and Cape Town, 1983); *Genealogies of Old South African Families*, vol. III, S–Z (Cape Town, 1966).

[34] See Shell, *Children of Bondage*, p. 432.

[35] Sheila Patterson, 'Some Speculations on the Status and Role of the Free People of Colour in the Western Cape', in Meyer Fortes and Sheila Patterson, eds, *Studies in African Social Anthropology* (London, New York and San Francisco, 1975), p. 172.

[36] See Shell, *Children of Bondage*, p. 393.

[37] Ibid. p. 134.

[38] For the most comprehensive analysis of the history of slave orphans, and orphan estimates for the child slave population at the Cape in the early nineteenth century, see Shell, *Children of Bondage* pp. 85–134.

[39] Jacques Rousseau, *Discourse on the Origin of Inequality* (Indianapolis and Cambridge, 1992).

[40] Denis Diderot, 'Hottentot', *Encylopédie*, vol. 7, pp. 320–21.

[41] See William B. Cohen, *The French Encounter with Africans: White Response to Blacks, 1530–1880* (Bloomington, 1980)

[42] John Campbell, *Travels in South Africa Undertaken at the Request of the Missionary Society* (London, 1815), p. 25.

[43] Ibid., pp. 88–9.

[44] See Shell, *Children of Bondage*, pp. 304–5.

[45] *Will of Hendrik Cesars en Anna Catharina Staal.* The marriage registers of St George's cathedral start in 1806, after Hendrik and Anna were married.

[46] See Jane Sales, *Mission Stations and the Coloured Communities of the Eastern Cape 1800–1852* (Cape Town and Rotterdam, 1975), p. 34.

[47] See the Colonial Office correspondence concerning Dunlop CO22, 1810, Government Archives, Cape Town.

[48] 'Examination of the Hottentot Venus'.

[49] Ibid.

[50] Army Paylists, WO12/9399 and WO12/9400, National Archives, London.

[51] *Morning Herald*, 29 November 1810, p. 3.

[52] Cuvier, *Report*.

[53] See Major G. Tylden, *The Armed Forces of South Africa*, City of Johannesburg Africana Museum Frank Connock Publication No. 2 (Johannesburg, 1982).

[54] William Jones to Rev. B. E. Sparke, Cape Town, 30 Sept 1796, Bowyer Sparke Papers, Norfolk Record Office, UPC, 316/1.

[55] Ibid.

[56] Ibid.

[57] 'Examination of the Hottentot Venus'.

4 STOWAWAY

[1] See Sampie Terreblanche, *A History of Inequality in South Africa 1652–2002* (Scottsville, 2002), pp. 181–5.

[2] Ibid. pp. 183–4.

[3] Sir Edward Hyde East, 'The Case of the Hottentot Venus', *Reports of Cases Argued and Determined in the Court of King's Bench*, vol. 13 (London, 1811), p. 195.

[4] *African Court Calendar* (Cape Town: Government Printing Office, 1810), Z/1 1/12, Government Archives, Cape Town.

[5] Colonel William Johnston, ed., *Roll of Commissioned Officers in the Medical Service of the British Army Who Served on Full Pay within the Period between the Accession of George II and the Formation of the Royal Army Medical Corps*, 20 June 1727 to 23 June 1898 (Aberdeen, 1917), p. 97.

[6] *African Court Calendar* (Cape Town, 1808, 1809, 1810), Government Archives, Cape Town, ZI/1/12; George McCall Theal, *Records of the Cape Colony*, vol. 8 (Cape Town, 1901), p. 140; Percy Laidler and Michael Gelfland, *South Africa, Its Medical History, 1652–1898* (Cape Town, 1971), p. 237.

[7] C. G. Hohne to His Excellency, Dupré, Earl Caledon, Governor of the Cape, 24 June 1810, CO2450, section 8, no. 16, Government Archives, Cape Town.

[8] Theal, *Records of the Cape Colony*, vol. 8, p. 140.

[9] Dr Hussey to HM Fiscal J. van Ryneveld, 1 and 8 March 1808, CO22, no. 13, Government Archives, Cape Town.

[10] Dr Hussey to HM Fiscal J. van Ryneveld, 2 December 1808, Government Archives, CO22, no. 13, Cape Town.

[11] Memorial of A. Dunlop to His Excellency, Dupré, Earl of Caledon, Governor and Commander in Chief of the Cape of Good Hope, and Its Dependencies, CO3875, vol. 1, 1810, no. 79, Government Archives, Cape Town.

[12] In 1806 the value of 1 rix-dollar was 4 English shillings. Over the next nineteen years, the value declined to 1 shilling and sixpence by 1825. Of course money conversions over time are highly unreliable; however, a working equivalent of an 1800 sum in the early twenty-first century can be roughly gauged by multiplying by between sixty and eighty.

[13] William Hussey MD to Captain Forster, 25 January 1810, CO22, no. 13, Government Archives, Cape Town.

[14] Both quotes are from General Grey to Lord Caledon, 26 January, 1810, CO22, no. 13, Government Archives, Cape Town.

[15] For a fuller account of this history, see Patricia Fara, *Sex, Botany and Empire*: (Cambridge *The Story of Carl Linneaeus and Joseph Banks*, 2003).

[16] See Shell, *Children of Bondage*, pp. 85–134.

[17] This history of interracial relationships has been extensively documented. For a recent fictional treatment reliably drawn from historical fact, see Dan Sleigh, *Islands* (London, 2004).

[18] Henry Alexander to Alexander Dunlop, 5 February, 1810, Lord Caledon Letter Book July 19th 1809 to January 25th 1810, p. 410, CO4827, Government Archives, Cape Town.

[19] Alexander Dunlop to Lord Caledon, 16 March, 1810, with enclosure from Thomas Ord, Custom House, CO22, 1810, no. 29, Government Archives, Cape Town.

[20] Alexander Dunlop to Henry Alexander, 7 March 1810, CO22, no. 25, 1810, Government Archives, Cape Town.

[21] *Cape Town Gazette, & African Advertiser*, 5/217 (10 March 1810); Records of Arrivals in Table Bay, PC3/1, Government Archives, Cape Town.

[22] Henry Alexander to Alexander Dunlop, Lord Caledon Letter Book February 24th 1810 to December 31st 1810, p. 48, CO4828, Government Archives, Cape Town.

[23] Both citations are from *Will of Hendrik Cesars en Anna Catharina Staal*.

[24] *Cape Town Gazette, & African Advertiser*, 5/221 (April 1810), p. 1.

[25] Royal Navy Ship Records, Navy Lists. The *Diadem*'s remaining musters for the period are at the National Archive, Kew, ADM37/4993 and ADM37/2754.

[26] Percy Byshe Shelley, 'The Witch of Atlas' (1820).

[27] See 'The Cameleopardalis', *Sporting Magazine*, XXXVVII, 218 (November 1810), pp. 81–2.

[28] The musters begin again on 20 June 1810, when the *Diadem* began wages and sea-victualling at Chatham; see ADM37/2754.

[29] *Examiner*, no. 152, 28 November p. 768.

[30] 'Examination of the Hottentot Venus', pt IV.

[31] Ibid.

[32] Table Mountain is 1,086 metres above sea level.

5 VENUS RISING

[1] Royal Navy Ship Records, Navy List, ADM37/2754, National Archive, Kew.

[2] Arthur Irwin Dasent, *The History of St James's Square and the Foundation of the West End of London* (London, 1895).

[3] H. Barton-Baker, *Stories of the Streets of London* (London, 1899); John Thomas Smith, *An Antiquarian Ramble in the Streets of London*, ed. Charles Mackay, vol. 1 (London, 1846), p. 18.

[4] See Nicholas Thomas, *Discoveries: The Voyages of Captain Cook* (London, 2003); Fara, *Sex, Botany and Empire*.

[5] Richard Altick, *The Shows of London* (Cambridge, MA, 1978), p. 235.

[6] Deposition to the Court of the King's Bench by William Bullock, 21 November 1810, PRO, KB 1/36, pt 4.

[7] Ibid.

[8] Ibid.

[9] Ibid.

[10] Ibid.

[11] Ibid.

[12] See 'Examination of the Hottentot Venus' affidavit.

[13] Altick, *The Shows of London*, p. 235.

[14] *A Companion to Mr Bullock's Museum, Containing a Brief Description of upwards of 7000 Natural and Foreign Curiosities* (London Reynell, 1810), British Library, Mic.A.12582 (3).

[15] Altick, *The Shows of London*, p. 237. Altick's account of Bullock

corrects the many factual errors regarding him and his museums contained in the first *Dictionary of National Biography*.

[16] *A Companion to Mr Bullock's Museum.*

[17] Deposition to the Court of the King's Bench by William Bullock.

[18] Percival Kirby, 'The Hottentot Venus', *Africana Notes and News*, VI/3 (June 1949), p. 56.

[19] Andrew Gage and William Stearn, *A Bicentenary History of The Linnean Society of London* (London, 1988), p. 196.

[20] See Altick, *The Shows of London*, pp. 269, 273.

[21] See Leslie Fiedler, *Freaks: Myths and Images of the Secret Self* (Harmondsworth, 1981); Altick, *The Shows of London*.

[22] This instrument was known to the Khoisan as a *mamokhorang*; Europeans described it as a Jew's harp.

[23] Cuvier, *Report on Observations Made on the Body of a Woman* (1817).

[24] *Punch*, 4 September 1847, cited in Altick, *The Shows of London*.

[25] Lysons, *Collectanea* vol. II.

[26] See Altick, *The Shows of London*; Mrs Anne Mathews, *Memoirs of Charles Mathews, Comedian*, vol. IV (London, 1839), pp. 133–7.

[27] Smith, *An Antiquarian Ramble* vol. I, p. 28.

[28] Ibid. p. 27.

[29] See Hilary Mantel, *The Giant O'Brien* (London, 1998); Altick, *The Shows of London*.

[30] Kirby, 'The Hottentot Venus', p. 57.

[31] This and the previous citation are from 'Examination of the Hottentot Venus'.

[32] This was Aristotle's description of the female pudenda. See Fiedler, *Freaks*, p. 138.

[33] Smith, 'Still More About The Hottentot Venus'.

[34] 'The Female Hottentot', *Examiner* [October 21st, 1810], p. 653.

[35] Cuvier, *Report On Observations*.

[36] Candace Allen, *Valaida: A Novel* (London, 2004), p. 159.

[37] See Peter Fryer, *Staying Power: The History of Black People in Britain* (London, 1984).

[38] In 1772 the Lord Chief Justice's court accepted a figure of 15,000

black people in Britain. Granville Sharp thought the number was nearer 20,000. See Paul Edwards and James Walvin, *Black Personalities in the Era of the Slave Trade* (London, 1983). Peter Fryer suggests a more conservative figure of 10,000; see *Staying Power*, p. 235.

[39] *Morning Herald*, 12 December 1810, p. 3.

[40] Yvette Abrahams has cogently argued the significance of this. In so doing she has effectively challenged recent academic work that mistakenly seeks to prove that Saartjie was never seen as an erotic object by white culture, only as gross and abject. This misreading results from scholarship that focuses on sources from élite travel accounts, ethnography and anthropology while ignoring contemporary press and popular-cultural sources. See Yvette Abrahams, 'Images of Sara Bartman: Sexuality, Race, and Gender in Early-Nineteenth-Century Britain', in Ruth Roach Pierson and Nupur Chaudhuri, eds, *Nation, Empire, Colony: Historicizing Gender and Race* (Bloomington and Indianapolis, 1998), pp. 225–36.

[41] I am indebted to diverse sources for these perspectives, including Josephine Baker, Florence Mills, Miriam Makeba, Brenda Fassie and J Lo. See also Candace Allen's fictionalisation of the life of Valaida Snow, *Valaida*, and Andrea Stuart, *Showgirls* (London, 1996).

[42] See Altick, *The Shows of London*, pp. 268–87.

[43] *Morning Herald*, 23 November 1810, p. 3.

[44] This and previous citation are from *Satirist, or, Monthly Meteor*, VII/3, 1 November 1810, pp. 424–7.

[45] See Anne McClintock, *Imperial Leather: Race, Gender and Sexuality in the Colonial Conquest* (New York and London, 1995).

[46] *Satirist, or, Monthly Meteor*, VII/3, 1 November 1810, pp. 424–7.

[47] Ibid.

[48] Ibid.

[49] *Morning Post*, 9 November 1810, p. 3.

[50] Ibid.

[51] 'Examination of the Hottentot Venus'.

6 FREEWOMAN OR SLAVE?

[1] *Examiner*, 14 October 1810, p. 9.

[2] Ibid.

[3] *Examiner*, 9 October 1810, p. 653.

[4] *Examiner*, 14 October 1810, p. 9.

[5] Ibid.

[6] Ibid.

[7] Ibid.

[8] For audience complicity with Cesars's strategy for dealing with this episode, see *Examiner*, 14 October 1810, p. 9.

[9] 'The Female Hottentot', 'Humanitas' to the editor, *Examiner*, 21 October 1810, p. 669.

[10] 'The Hottentot Venus', *Sporting Magazine*, 37/218 (November 1810), pp. 81–2.

[11] Ibid.

[12] Cited in Hugh Thomas, *The History of the Atlantic Slave Trade, 1440–1870* (London, 1997), p. 556.

[13] Report of the Committee of the African Institution, General Meeting, 15 July 1807, Rules and Regulations, then adopted as constitution for the society, 1807, Freemasons' Hall, Queen Street, Lincoln's Inn Fields, British Library, T87, p. 28–9.

[14] Ibid.

[15] Other founder-members included Lord Headley, Nicholas Vansittard, Sir Philip Francis, Sir Samuel Romilly, the Viscounts Howick and Valenta, and the Duke of Montague.

[16] George Harrison, 'Some Remarks on a Communication from William Roscoe to the Duke of Gloucester, March 20, 1809, as Stated in the Appendix of the Third Report of the African Institution' (London, 1810), BL 899 c22, p. 7.

[17] Ibid., p. 5.

[18] Thomas, *The Slave Trade*, p. 562.

[19] Such as, in 1814, rescuing a West Indian apprentice who had

been found chained to his master's table and treated appallingly. See Fryer, *Staying Power*, p. 228.

20 See Thomas, *The Slave Trade*, p. 535.

21 Ibid., p. 412.

22 Ibid., p. 734.

23 *Morning Chronicle*, 12 October 1810, p. 3.

24 Sworn Affidavit of Zachary Macaulay, Thomas Gisborne Babington and Peter van Wageninge, Serjeant's Inn, Chancery Lane, London, 17 October 1810, KB/36, PRO, Kew, London.

25 Ibid.

26 *Morning Chronicle*, 12 October 1810, p. 3.

27 This and previous citations are from Ernest Marshall Howse, *Saints in Politics: The 'Clapham Sect' and the Growth of Freedom* (London 1952), p. 22.

28 Maurice Quinlan, *Victorian Prelude: A History of English Manners (1700–1830)* (London 1965), pp. 203–4.

29 Ibid. pp. 205–6.

30 See Catherine Hall, *White, Male and Middle Class: Explorations in Feminism and History* (Cambridge and Oxford, 1998).

31 Bernth Lindfors, '"The Hottentot Venus": and Other African Attractions in Nineteenth-century England', *Australasian Drama Studies*, 1/2 (1982), p. 84.

32 All citations are from Sworn Affidavit of Zachary Macaulay.

33 *Morning Chronicle*, 13 October, 1810, p. 3.

34 Ibid.

35 Ibid.

36 Act for the Abolition of the Slave Trade, 25 March 1807 (London, 1807).

37 Ibid.

38 Ibid.

39 *Morning Chronicle*, 17 October 1810, p. 3.

40 Ibid.

41 Ibid.

42 *Morning Chronicle*, 23 October 1810, p. 4.

[43] Ibid.

[44] 'Humanitas' to the editor, *Examiner*, 21 October 1810, p. 669.

[45] Ibid.

[46] *Morning Chronicle*, 23 October 1810, p. 4.

[47] Deposition to the Court of the King's Bench by William Bullock.

[48] *Morning Chronicle*, 23 October 1810, p. 4.

[49] *Morning Chronicle*, 24 October, 1810, p. 3.

[50] *A Ballad: The Storie of the Hottentot Ladie and Her Lawfull Knight, Who Essaied to Release Her out of Captivitie, and What My Lordes the Judges Did Therein* (London, 1810); see Daniel Lysons, *Collectanea; or a Collection of Advertisements and Paragraphs from Newspapers, Relating to Various Subjects*, vol. Iii, unpub. scrapbook, British Library.

[51] Ibid.

7 THE CASE OF THE HOTTENTOT VENUS

[1] Le Blanc, appointed Justice of the King's Bench in 1799, was a senior barrister.

[2] The writ of habeas corpus ('that you have the body') is a process for securing the liberty of the subject by affording an effective means of immediate release from unlawful or unjustifiable detention whether in prison or in private custody. It is a prerogative writ by which the Sovereign has a right to inquire into the causes for which any of her subjects are deprived of their liberty. By it the High Court and the judges of that court, at the instance of the subject aggrieved, command the production of that subject, and inquire into the cause of his imprisonment. If there is no legal justification for the detention, the party is ordered to be released. See Halsbury's *Laws of England*, 4th edn, 2001 reissue, vol. 1 (1) (London, 2001), pp. 366–402; Earl Jowitt, *Dictionary of English Law* (London, 1959), pp. 886–7.

[3] *Morning Chronicle*, 24 October 1810

[4] 'The Female Hottentot', *Examiner*. Sunday 21 October, p. 669.

[5] Sworn Affidavit of Zachary Macaulay . . .

[6] 'The Female Hottentot', p. 653. The attribution of this letter is uncertain. It is not Macaulay (see his response in the following issue, 21 October, p. 669) but the concluding remarks regarding the benefits of a missionary education and voluntary repatriation indicate clearly someone from, or closely allied to, the Clapham Sect. The most likely candidates are Haldane and Hannah More.

[7] This and previous citations from Sworn Affidavit of Zachary Macaulay . . .

[8] Ibid.

[9] *Morning Chronicle*, 13 October, 1810, p. 3.

[10] 'The Female Hottentot', p. 669.

[11] See Thomas, *The Slave Trade*.

[12] Letter to *Examiner*, 21 October 1810, p. 669.

[13] See Elizabeth Elbourne, '"To Colonise the Mind": Evangelical Missionaries in Britain and the Eastern Cape, 1740–1837' (DPhil thesis, University of Oxford, 1992)

[14] Ibid.

[15] *The Diary of Joseph Farington*, vol. VI, April 1803–December 1804 (New Haven and London, 1979), pp. 2186–7.

[16] For the history of the King's Bench court and its role in the machinery of justice, see Stanley de Smith and Rodney Brazier, *Constitutional and Administrative Law* (London, 1998), pp. 359–87; A. W. Bradley and K. D. Ewing, *Constitutional and Administrative Law* (Harlow, 1997), pp. 408–55.

[17] The Court of the King's Bench, the supreme common-law court of England, is headed by the King/Queen or his/her personal representative, in this case the Attorney General, the only person who could initiate legal proceedings on behalf of the Crown. For the origins and history of the Court of the King's Bench, see May, *Constitutional History*, vol. I (London, NYC, and Bombay, 1896); M.M. Knappen, *Constitutional and Legal History of England* (New York, 1942); and John Hamilton Baker, *An Introduction to English Legal History* (London, 1990).

[18] See 'Report of the Committee of the African Institution, General Meeting July 15th 1807, Rules and Regulations, then Adopted as Constitution for the Society; London, 1807, Freemason's Hall, Queen Street, Lincoln's Inn Fields', British Library, T87.

[19] See Ben Wilson, *The Laughter of Triumph: William Hone and the Fight for the Free Press* (London, 2005), p. 76.

[20] 'Law Report', *Times*, 26 November 1810, p. 3.

[21] Unless otherwise cited, this account of the court case and all citations for the hearings of 26 and 29 November are drawn from the following sources: 'The Case of the Hottentot Venus', *The English Reports*, vol. CIV, King's Bench Division, XXXIII, reprint edn (Oxford, 1980), pp. 344–5; Sir Edward Hyde East, 'The Case of the Hottentot Venus, Saturday November 24th, 1810', *Reports of Cases Argued and Determined in the Court of King's Bench*, vol. 13 (London, 1811) pp. 195–6; 'Law Report: Court of King's Bench, Saturday, November 24th: The Hottentot Venus', *Times*, 26 November 1810, p. 3, and 29 November 1810, p. 3; 'Law Intelligence: Court of King's Bench, Saturday November 24th: The Hottentot Venus', *Morning Chronicle*, 26 November 1810, p. 3, and 29 November 1810, p. 3; 'Law Report: Court of King's Bench, November 24th: The Hottentot Venus', *Morning Herald*, 26 November 1810, p. 3, and 29 November 1810, p. 3; 'The Hottentot Venus', *Examiner*, 21 October 1810, p. 669. Manuscript copies of the affidavits of Saartjie Baartman, William Bullock, Zachary Macaulay, Thomas Babington, Peter van Wageninge and Alexander Dunlop are in the archive of the King's Bench, The National Archives, Kew, London.

[22] Davis, *The Problem of Slavery*, p. 472.

[23] Ibid. p. 473.

[24] Ibid.

[25] See Somerset v Stewart, 14 May 1772, *The English Reports*, vol. XCVIII, King's Bench Division, XXVII (Oxford, 1909), pp. 499–510; Edmund Heward, *Lord Mansfield* (Chichester and London, 1979), p. 143.

[26] See Rachel Holmes, 'Rainbow Afrikaans', *Prospect*, 98 (May 2004), pp. 78–9.

[27] Henry Alexander to Alexander Dunlop, Lord Caledon Letter Book, February 24th 1810 to December 31st 1810, p. 48, Government Archives, Cape Town, CO4828.

[28] This and all proceeding references to the contract are from Prof. Verneau's translation, 'Le centième anniversaire de la mort de Saartjie Bartmann', *L'Anthropologie*, Volume 27 (1916), p. 178.

[29] 'Examination of the Hottentot Venus' affidavit, 27 November 1810, KB1/36, part 4, King's Bench, Court Records, National Archives (TNA)

[30] John Lord Campbell, *The Lives of the Chief Justices of England*, vol. 3 (London, 1857), p. 161.

[31] 'The Case of the Hottentot Venus', *The English Reports*, vol. CIV, King's Bench Division, XXXIII, reprint edn (Oxford, 1980), pp. 344–5; Campbell, *The Lives of the Chief Justices of England*, p. 1661.

[32] Charles Dickens, *The Pickwick Papers* (Oxford, 1987), pp. 466–7.

[33] Ibid.

[34] Davis, *The Problem of Slavery*, p. 489.

[35] Ibid.

[36] Ibid.

[37] The paternalism and utilitarian racism of this legislation can be seen from its opening justification: '. . . for the benefit of this Colony at large, it is necessary, that not only the Individuals of the Hottentot Nation, in the same manner as the other Inhabitants, should be subject to proper regularity in regard to their places of abode and occupation, but also, that they should find an encouragement, for preferring entering the service of the Inhabitants, to leading an indolent life, by which they are rendered useless both for themselves, and the community at large' (1 November 1809, Official Proclamations, Caledon Papers, Government Archives, Cape Town, ZI1/1).

[38] They would first have had to prod the Crown to prosecute, and

on their refusal obtained a 'nolle prosequi' ('we shall no longer prosecute'), an entry made on the record by the prosecution stating that they would no longer pursue the matter – essentially an admission that some aspect of the case had fallen apart. They could then have instituted a private prosecution. However, the case on behalf of the African Institution lacked the surety of being able to prove beyond reasonable doubt, and the jury might have been inclined to be sympathetic with the accused and so acquit. Given these potential complexities, there was far more control and security in the African Institution pursuing the habeas corpus procedure.

[39] Angela Carter, *Black Venus* (London, 1985), p. 20. In Carter's tale of Jeanne Duval, Baudelaire's mistress, Duval contemplates her status as a Parisienne prostitute: 'Seller and commodity in one, a whore is her own investment in the world and so she must take care of herself.'

8 CACHE-SEXE

[1] *Morning Post*, 30 April 1811, p.1.

[2] Bernth Lindfors, 'The Afterlife of the Hottentot Venus', *Neohelican: Acta Comparat Litteraraum Universarum*, Volume 16, No. 2, September 1989, 293–301, p. 298

[3] Bernth Lindfors, 'The Bottom Line: African Caricature in Georgian England', *World Literature Written in English*, 24/1 (1984), pp. 43–51, esp. pp. 49–50.

[4] 'The Humours of Bartlemy Fair', *The Universal Songster* (London, n. d.), vol. I, pp. 118–19.

[5] See Smith, 'Still More about the Hottentot Venus', p. 97.

[6] The Diary of Reverend Dr Laurence Hayes Halloran' cited in Theal, *Records of the Cape Colony from 1798 to 1828*, vol. VIII (London, 1897–1905), p. 140; see also Philip, *British Residents at the Cape*, p. 162.

[7] Mrs G. Linnaeus Banks, *The Manchester Man* (Manchester, 1991), p. 22.

[8] Brookes's avid and eclectic collecting provides a hint as to his awareness of The Hottentot Venus. After his death, some were shocked to discover his salacious bibliophilic preferences: 'Although he brought together a large library, he was entirely deficient in the finer instincts of the bibliomaniac, and nothing could be more tasteless than his fashion of illustrating his books with tawdry and worthless engravings.' In other words, he collected pornography.

[9] Banks, *The Manchester Man* (1991), p. 23.

[10] Register of the Collegiate and Parish Church of Christ, Manchester, 1 December 1811

[11] *Cowdroys Manchester Gazette, and Weekly Advertiser*, 14 December 1811, p. 4.

[12] Maurice Lenihan, *Limerick: Its History and Antiquities, Ecclesiastical, Civil and Military* (1886; Cork, 1967), p. 416; Bill Rolston and Michael Shannon, *Encounters: How Racism Came to Ireland* (Belfast, 2002), p. 70.

[13] Johnston, *Roll of Commissioned Officers*, p. 97. Dunlop's Return of Service was destroyed in bomb damage to the Public Records Office during World War II.

[14] Altick, *The Shows of London*, p. 240.

[15] Ibid.

[16] See Altick's comprehensive account of the carriage exhibition, drawing from the *Repository of Arts, Literature & Fashion* (1816), and Elizabeth Longford, *Wellington: The Years of the Sword* (London, 1969) pp. 239–41.

[17] The appearance of Saartjie's poster image in Cruikshank and Rowlandson's cartoons of the exhibition of Napoleon's carriage has led to the oft-repeated but erroneous claim that she exhibited at the Egyptian Hall.

[18] Frank McLynn, *Napoleon: A Biography* (London, 1997), p. 265.

[19] Agreed by the allies on 1 March 1814, the Treaty of Chaumont bound the anti-Napoleon alliance for twenty years, and stated the objectives of victory as 'an enlarged and independent Holland, a confederated Germany, an independent Switzerland, a free Spain

under a Bourbon dynasty, and the restitution of the Italian states'. See Asa Briggs, *The Age of Improvement* (London, 1959), p. 159.

[20] See Hervé Le Guyader, *Geoffroy Saint-Hilaire: A Visionary Naturalist* (Chicago, 2004).

[21] As described by Elizabeth Barrett Browning in *Aurora Leigh*, bk VI (see, Elizabeth Barrett Browning, *Aurora Leigh*, ed. Margaret Reynolds [London, 1996], p. 184).

[22] See Browning, *Aurora Leigh* p. 185.

[23] Ibid.

[24] The Jardin des Plantes and Jardin du Roi refer to the same institution. Between 1793 and 1848, depending upon the changing political fortunes of the Republic and the Monarchy, the institution was known either as Jardin des Plantes or Jardin du Roi. It was thus known by both names in the period of political transition during which Saartjie was in Paris.

[25] Henry Taylor to André Thouin, 10 September 1814, *Correspondence et comptes rendus des assemblées des professeurs*, National Archives, Paris. For a full transcription of the letter, see Gerard Badou, *L'Enigme de la Vénus hottentote* (Paris, 2000), p. 110.

[26] Badou, *L'Enigme*, p. 115.

[27] See Franck Bourdier, 'Georges Cuvier', in Charles Coulston Gillispie, ed., *Dictionary of Scientific Biography* (New York, 1972), vol. III, p. 524.

[28] See Bourdier, 'Georges Cuvier', p. 524.

[29] Strother points out that François Le Vaillant was the only traveller to write on the people he labelled the Hauzanana (a San group) in relation to steatopygia. See Z. S. Strother, 'Display of the Body Hottentot', in Bernth Lindfors, ed., *Africans on Stage: Studies in Ethnological Show Business* (Bloomington and Indianapolis, 1999), p. 33. This awareness of the body of travel writing about the Cape demonstrated in the Hottentot Venus advertisement raises interesting questions about their sources.

[30] *Affiches, annonces et avis divers ou Journal Général de France*, 18 September 1814, p. 15, Bibliothèque Nationale. The souvenir

poster on offer was probably the ubiquitous acquatint by Lewis.

[31] *Affiches, annonces et avis divers ou Journal Général de France*, 27 January 1815, p.12.

[32] *Affiches, annonces et avis divers ou Journal Général de France*, 18 September 1814, p. 15.

[33] Ibid.

[34] *Journal général de France*, 22 September 1814, p. 13.

[35] 'La Vénus hottentote'.

[36] Ibid.

[37] Ibid.

[38] Ibid.

[39] Ibid.

[40] Kirby, 'More about the Hottentot Venus'.

[41] Ibid.

[42] See Strother, 'Display of the Body Hottentot'. Strother offers a concise reading of the racist negation of Saartjie as an object of desire in this cruel and misogynistic comedy.

[43] *Journal général de France*, 21 November 1814, pp. 3–4.

[44] *Journal des debats politiques et littéraires*, 21 November 1814, pp. 3–4.

[45] Andrea Stuart, *Showgirls* (London, 1996), p. 85.

[46] Ibid., p. 104.

[47] For an excellent analysis of how Saartjie's reception presaged Josephine's, see Stuart, *Showgirls*, pp. 78–80.

[48] See Wood, *The Josephine Baker Story*, p. 105; Stuart, *Showgirls*, pp. 78–80.

[49] See announcement in the *Gazette de France*, 28 October 1814.

[50] McLynn, *Napoleon*, pp. 606–7.

[51] Last Will and Testament of Anna Catharina Staal, Widow of the Late Hendrick Cesars, Resident of Papendorp, 2 August 1841, Government Archives, Cape Town.

[52] *Affiches, annonces et avis divers ou Journal général de France*, 22 January 1815. See also 24, 26 and 27 January.

[53] Ibid.

[54] *Journal général de France*, 23 January 1815.

[55] See Kirby, 'The "Hottentot Venus" of the Musée de L'Homme, Paris', pp. 319–22.

[56] *Affiches, annonces et avis divers ou Journal général de France*, 22 January 1815. See also 24, 26, 27 and 28 January, and 1–8 February.

9 PAINTED FROM THE NUDE

[1] Records of this event emerged through scientific journals in the early twentieth century on the centenary of Saartjie's death. It was first referred to in Verneau, 'Le centième anniversaire de la mort de Saartjie Bartmann', and Jean Avalon, 'Saartjie, La "Vénus Hottentote"', *Aesculape: Revue mensuelle illustrée – Organe officiel de la Société Internationale d'Histoire de la Medicine*, vol. 16, 1926.

[2] Cuvier, *Report on Observations.*

[3] These diary entries were discovered by Heather Ewing during research for her book on James Smithson, founder of the Smithsonian Museum. I am very grateful for her generosity in sharing these original references.

[4] Blagden Diary, 9 October 1814, Royal Society Archives, 1814, 1815.

[5] These citations all from Bladgen Diary, 10 January 1815, Royal Society Archives.

[6] Etienne Geoffroy Saint-Hilaire to M. Boucheseiche, 16 February 1815, Archives de la Préfecture de Police de Paris. For a full transcript, see Gerard Badou, *L'énigme de la Vénus Hottentote* (Paris, 2000), p. 133.

[7] See Anne Fausto-Sterling, 'Gender, Race, and Nation: The Comparative Anatomy of "Hottentot" Women in Europe, 1815–1817', in Jennifer Terry and Jacqueline Urla, eds, *Deviant Bodies: Critical Perspectives on Difference in Science and Popular Culture* (Bloomington and Indianapolis, 1995), pp. 19–47, esp. p. 23.

[8] See Michael Allin, *Zarafa: A Giraffe's True Story* (London, 1998), pp. 127–9.

[9] For documentation of the animals kept in the zoo in 1815, see Joseph-Philippe-François Deleuze, *Histoire et description du Muséum Royal d'Histoire Naturelle* (Paris, 1823), pp. 105–6.

[10] See Deleuze, *Histoire et description*, p. 106.

[11] 'It is related that a naturalist once discovered in a mine what seemed to be a new species of plant, but when transplanted on the surface of the earth it turned out to be a common *tansy* – an abnormal habitat had altered its appearance past recognition' (William Payne, translator's introduction to Rousseau's *Emile* (1892), p. xxxvi.

[12] See Angela Carter, *Nights at the Circus* (London, 1994), p. 7. Carter's heroine Fevvers, the 'Cockney Venus', is inspired by Saartjie.

[13] For 'freaks' and the science of teratology, see Fiedler, *Freaks*. For Saint-Hilaire and the development of teratology, see Franck Bourdier, 'Etienne Geoffroy Saint-Hilaire', in Fischer and Haberlandt, eds, *Dictionary of Scientific Biography*, vol. V, pp. 355–8; and Allin, *Zarafa*, pp. 134–5.

[14] The separation of art and science as a recent phenomenon has been widely documented and debated. For an intervention focused on this relationship at the Jardin des Plantes and the Museum of Natural History, see Barbara Stafford, *Artful Science* (Cambridge, MA, 1994), pp. 254–79

[15] See Deleuze, *Histoire et description*, p. 174.

[16] Henri de Blainville, 'Sur une femme de la race hottentote', *Bulletin des sciences par la Société Philomathique de Paris* (Paris, 1816), pp. 183–90.

[17] See John Lempriere, *Lempriere's Classical Dictionary of Proper Names Mentioned in Ancient Authors Writ Large, With Chronological Table* (London, 1986).

[18] *The Journals of Captain Cook 1768–1779*, ed. Philip Edwards (London, 1999), p. 327. For a discussion of the apron in general and Saartjie in particular, see Carmel Schrire, 'Native Views of Western

Eyes', in Pippa Skotnes, ed., *Miscast: Negotiating the Presence of the Bushmen* (Cape Town, 1996), pp. 343–53, Carmel Schrire *Digging through Darkness: Chronicles of an Archaeologist* (Charlottesville and London, 1995), pp. 176–8.

[19] R. Raven-Hart, *Before Van Riebeeck: Callers at South Africa from 1488 to 1652* (Cape Town, 1967), p. 152.

[20] Cited in Strother, 'Display of the Body Hottentot', p. 21.

[21] Ibid., pp. 21–2.

[22] George Stocking, 'French Anthropology in 1800', *Isis*, vol. 55, 2, No. 180 (July 1964), pp. 134–50.

[23] De Blainville, 'Sur une femme de la race hottentote'.

[24] Ibid.

[25] Ibid.

[26] Ibid.

[27] Ibid.

[28] Cuvier, *Report on Observations*.

[29] See Kenneth Clark, *The Nude* (Harmondsworth, 1956), p. 64.

[30] See Hugh Honour, *The Image of the Black in Western Art*, vol. IV (Cambridge, MA, 1989), pp. 54–5.

[31] *Bulletin des sciences par la Société Philomathique de Paris.*

[32] De Blainville, 'Sur une femme de la race hottentote'; Cuvier, *Report on Observations*.

[33] 'And you should fear the vengeance of gods / Venus who hates a stony heart, the wrath / The unforgetting wrath of Nemesis' (Ovid, *Metamorphoses* [Oxford, 1986], xiv. 679–710, p. 346).

10 THE DEATH OF VENUS

[1] See Roy Porter, *The Greatest Benefit to Mankind: A Medical History of Humanity from Antiquity to the Present* (London, 1997), p. 321.

[2] Cuvier, *Report on Observations*.

[3] The most famous of course being Joseph Merrick, the Elephant Man.

[4] See Badou, *L'Enigme*, p. 152.

[5] Geoffroy Saint-Hilaire to Prefect of Police, Saturday, 30 December 1815, *Collections officielles des ordonnances de Police: 1800–1848*, Paris Police Archives. See Badou, *L'Enigme*, pp. 152, 154.

[6] See Badou, *L'Enigme*, pp. 152, 154.

[7] *Collections officielles des ordonnances de Police: 1800–1848*, Paris Police Archives.

[8] Pierre Gratiolet, 'Mémoire sure les plis cérébraux de l'homme et des primates', in Huxley's 1864 lecture series 'The Structure and Classification of the Mammalis', *Medical Times and Gazette* (October 1864).

[9] Huxley, 'The Structure and Classification of the Mammalis'.

[10] For Cuvier's use of the possessive when referring to Saartjie, see *Report on Observations*.

[11] Cited in Stocking, 'French Anthropology in 1800'. p. 142.

[12] Ibid.

[13] Ibid.

[14] Ibid.

[15] Ibid.

[16] 'Paris News: 30th December', and Obituary, *Journal général de France*, 31 December 1815.

[17] 'Paris News: 30th December', *Journal général de France*, 31 December 1815.

[18] '*Nouvelles de Paris: La Vénus hottentote est morte*', Obituary, 1 January 1816, p. 4.

[19] *Annales politiques, morales et littéraires*, 1 January 1816.

[20] See Saul Dubow, *Scientific Racism in Modern South Africa* (Cambridge, 1995), pp. 20–33; Schrire, 'Native Views of Western Eyes'; Schrire, *Digging through Darkness: Chronicles of an Archaeologist* (Charlottsville and London, 1995).

[21] Letter from 'A Man and a Christian', 16 October 1810, Lysons, *Collectanea*, vol. Iii, p. 102. Possible attributions include the black radical activist Robert Wedderburn, a proto-feminist and libertarian who took a hard line on the ill treatment of women.

[22] *Journal général de France*, 8 January 1816.

[23] Ibid.

[24] Ibid.

[25] *Mercure de France*, January 1816, p. 334.

[26] Cuvier, *Report on Observations*.

[27] See Sander Gilman, 'Black Bodies, White Bodies: Toward an Iconography of Female Sexuality in Late Nineteenth-Century Art, Medicine, and Literature', in Henry Louis Gates, Jr, ed., *'Race', Writing, and Difference* (Chicago, 1986), pp. 223–61. Strother argues, correctly, that a 'historical slippage' occurs in Gilman's analysis between 'the circumstances of Baartman's exhibition and its contemporary reception', because Gilman's interest is in the mid- to late nineteenth-century appropriation of her body for medical discourse rather than in her live exhibition. See Strother, 'Display of the Body Hottentot', pp. 38–9. However, the evidence from popular culture, rather than science, challenges Strother's thesis that Saartjie's exhibition was received as a neutralisation of desire, and 'comfortingly anti-erotic' (p. 40); Strother's analysis does not account for the relationship between abjection and lascivious desire.

[28] See Emile Zola, *Nana* (Paris, 1880), and as cited in Gilman, 'Black Bodies, White Bodies', p. 254.

[29] See Gilman, 'Black Bodies, White Bodies', p. 254; Honour, *The Image of the Black in Western Art*, vol. IV p. 235; Jill Matus, 'Blonde, Black and Hottentot Venus: Context and Critique in Angela Carter's "Black Venus",' *Studies in Short Fiction*, 28/4 (Fall 1991), pp. 467–76.

[30] Cuvier, *Report on Observations*.

[31] 'Variétés', *L'Ambigu*, 10 January 1816, pp. 38–40.

[32] Ibid.

[33] For the provenance of the Medici Venus, see Clark, *The Nude*, p. 370.

[34] See Alistair Horne, *The Seven Ages of Paris: Portrait of a City* (London, 2002); Hilaire Belloc, *Napoleon* (Hamburg, Paris and Bologna, 1933).

[35] Lysons, *Collectanea*, Vol III, p. 106.

[36] Richard Owen, *A Report to the Board of Curators of the Museum of the Royal College of Surgeons*, Royal College of Surgeons Library and Archives, Lincoln's Inn Fields, London RCS MS 275. L. 7. (1831), p. 8.

[37] Ibid., p. 7.

[38] Ibid., p. 10.

[39] Deleuze, *Histoire et description*, p. 660.

[40] Ibid.

[41] Ibid.

[42] Owen, *A Report to the Board*, p. 5.

[43] To keep warm while working, Cuvier carried his stove with him. See Fausto-Sterling, 'Gender, Race, and Nation', p. 32.

[44] See Mary Shelley, *Frankenstein* (London, 1992), p. 49. Shelley began writing *Frankenstein* in June 1816.

[45] Frédéric Cuvier, cited in Dorinda Outram, *Georges Cuvier: Science, Authority and Vocation in Post-Revolutionary France* (London & Dover, New Hampshire, 1984), p. 183.

[46] See A. B. Griffiths, *Biographies of Scientific Men* (London, 1912), p. 24.

[47] Contemporary commentators who believe that images of Saartjie should be the preserve of academic researchers should consider this history carefully. Doubtless some will be shocked or offended by the images, but many will learn from them.

[48] Griffiths, *Biographies of Scientific Men*, p. 24.

[49] Bourdier, 'Georges Cuvier'.

[50] Ibid.

[51] Fausto-Sterling, 'Gender, Race, and Nation', p. 44, n. 16.

[52] Edward Spitzka, cited in Fausto-Sterling, 'Gender, Race, and Nation', p. 44, n.16.

[53] Stephen Jay Gould, 'The Hottentot Venus', *The Flamingo's Smile: Reflections in Natural History* (New York, 1985), pp. 291–2.

[54] Ibid., p. 292.

[55] See Gilman, 'Black Bodies, White Bodies', p. 238.

[56] Cited in Schrire, *Digging through Darkness*, p. 179.

[57] Ibid.

[58] Jonathan Thompson, 'This Year's Must Have Cosmetic Surgery: The Beyoncé Nip and Butt', *Independent on Sunday*, 17 April 2005.

[59] Jeya Prakash, cited in Thompson, 'This Year's Must'.

[60] Schrire, *Digging through Darkness*, p. 183. Schrire's consummate counter-analysis of the history of racist ethnography of the Khoisan female body shows that Khoisan women laughed at the European travellers who bribed or cajoled them to raise their skirts because showing their genitals was the rudest insult imaginable in their culture – a point the European strangers eternally failed to understand (p. 180).

11 LAYING DOWN THE BONES

[1] Richard Owen's 1822 report to the Royal College of Surgeons confirms that Saartjie's remains were not yet on public display. No museum record has yet been discovered that confirms the exact date when Cuvier's collection went on public display.

[2] Phillip V. Tobias, 'Saartjie Baartman: Her Life, Her Remains, and the Negotiations for Their Repatriation from France to South Africa', *South African Journal of Science*, no. 98 (March – April 2002), pp. 107–10.

[3] Ibid.

[4] Gould, 'The Hottentot Venus', p. 291.

[5] Dr Ben Ngubane, 'Efforts to Repatriate Remains of Saartjie Baartman Continue', 10 October 2000; http://www.sabcnews.com/Article/0,1093,5652,00.html.

[6] See Ayesha Ismail, 'Victory as Griquas Gain First Nation Status', *Sunday Times* (Cape Town), 9 August 1998; http://www.suntimes.co.za/1998/08/09.news/cape/net07.1; and Resolutions as Agreed by Official and Associate Delegates to the National Khoisan Consultative Conference on Khoisan Diversity in National Unity held in Oudtshoorn, 29 March–1 April 2001, Urgent Anthropology,

http://www.und.ac.za.und/ccms/anthropology/urgent/khoisan. html. In 1997 the Western Cape legislature allocated a grant of 100,000 rands to Le Fleur's group to cover the costs of Saartjie's repatriation. During the same week that the UN accorded first-nation status to the Khoisan, a delegation representing Khoisan groups met with the Cape legislature to plan a campaign for the return of Saartjie's relics.

7 As Ngubane remarked, with pointed irony, so extensive is this plunder that 'if all these objects were to be repatriated to South Africa, it would be impossible for them to be properly accommodated, curated and handled within existing facilities' ('Efforts to Repatriate Remains').

8 Tobias, 'Saartjie Baartman', p. 109.

9 See SABC, 'Khoi Groups Claim to be Saartjie's Descendents', 6 August 2002; www.sabcnews.com/article/0, 1093, 40207,00; Zola Maseko and Gail Smith, *The Return of Sarah Baartman*, Black Roots Pictures, Brooklyn: First Run/Icarus Films, 2002).

10 Cited in Davies, *The Return of El Negro*, p. 229.

11 Interview with Brigitte Mabandla, 'Sarah Baartman Funeral', video footage, 9 August 2002, South African Broadcasting Corporation, 63323–4.

12 Maseko and Smith, *The Return of Sarah Baartman*.

13 See Davies, *The Return of El Negro*.

14 Chris McGreal, 'Coming Home', *Guardian*, 21 February 2002; http://education.guardian.co.uk/0, 3858, 4360082.00.html.

15 Ibid.

16 SABC, 'Hottentot Venus May Finally Come Home', 28 January 2002; http://www.sabcnews.com/article/0,1093,27402.00.html.

17 Ibid.

18 Cited in McGreal, 'Coming Home'.

19 Diana Ferrus, 'I Have Come to Take You Home – a Tribute to Saartjie Baartman', in Malika Conning Ndlovu, Deela Khan, Shelley Barry (eds.), *Ink@boilingpoint: A Selection of 21st Century Black Women's Writing from the Tip of Africa* (Cape Town, 2002).

[20] Maseko and Smith, *The Return of Sarah Baartman*.

[21] Author interview with Diana Ferrus, Cape Town, 19 February 2005.

[22] Thabo Mbeki, 'Speech at the Funeral of Sarah Baartman', Hankey, 9 August 2002; www.anc.org.za/ancdocs/history/mbeki/2002/tm0809.html.

[23] SABC, 'Saartjie Baartman to Be Enrobed', 3 August 2002; http://sabcnews.com/article/0,1093,39990, 00.html.

[24] Maseko and Smith, *The Return of Sarah Baartman*.

[25] Jackson Zweliyanyikima Vena at the Cory Library for Historical Research, University of Rhodes, is currently engaged in genealogical research in the Eastern Cape. I am grateful to him for sharing his knowledge on Saartjie's Eastern Cape origins, and his observations on the significance of her traditional burial rites.

[26] Refers to people of mixed Khoekhoen and European ancestry.

[27] Willa Boezak, cited in Caroline Hooper-Box, 'Baartman set for return to African soil', *Sunday Independent*, South Africa, 2 feb 2002; and see the www.ink.iol.co.3a.

[28] In Parliament, ANC MP Nosipho Ntwanambi condemned Saarjtie's exploitation and welcomed the restoration of her dignity. The burial of her remains, he said, 'would reflect the new non-racial and respectful South Africa'. Bridget Mabandla made a forceful demand for 'the continuation of the struggle and for the ultimate emancipation of women'. See SABC, 'Inhumane Suffering of Sarah Barmann Condemned', 7 August 2002; http://sabcnews.com/article/0,1093,40280,00.

[29] On the day of Saartjie's funeral, the Commission for Gender Equality organised a march in Pretoria to commemorate the 1956 women's demonstrations against the pass laws. Honouring Saartjie in their speeches, the protestors acknowledged the government's successes in addressing gender issues since 1994. However, they pointed out that there was still a great deal of work to be done, especially in tackling high rates of rape and abuse of women and children.

[30] The Saartjie Baartman Centre, located in Athlone, a township near Cape Town. Yvette Abrahams said, 'Women visiting here must be able to say I went to Sarah Bartmaan and she gave me shelter. What makes me proud is the way she lives in people's lives.' See SABC, 'Sarah Bartmann, Celebrated', 7 August 2002; http://sabc-news.com/article/1,093, 40224, 00.html.

[31] Press reports suggested that 7,000 people attended the funeral. From estimates of individuals who were there, and from film coverage, between 2,000 and 3,000 is more accurate.

[32] 'Sarah Baartman Funeral', 9 August 2002, South African Broadcasting Corporation, 63323–4.

[33] Ibid.

[34] Ibid.

[35] This and all subsequent references from Mbeki's speech are from 'Speech at the Funeral of Sarah Baartman'.

[36] Mbeki cited the following passage in his speech: 'The Negro race . . . is marked by black complexion, crisp woolly hair, compressed cranium and a flat nose. The projection of the lower parts of the face, and the thick lips, evidently approximate it to the monkey tribe: the hordes of which it consists have always remained in the most complete state of barbarism . . . These races with depressed and compressed skulls are condemned to a never-ending inferiority . . . Her moves had something that reminded one of the monkey and her external genitalia recalled those of the orang-utang' (Cuvier, *Report on Observations*). The global media constantly extracted and reproduced this quotation.

[37] See Neville Hoad, 'Thabo Mbeki's AIDS Blues: The Intellectual, The Archive, and the Pandemic', *Public Culture*, 17/(1) (2005), pp. 101–27. Hoad offers an insightful reading of how this episode raises questions about intention and audience when reproducing racist representation.

[38] Hoad, 'Thabo Mbeki's AIDS Blues'.

[39] Dr Mamphele Ramphele, 13th International AIDS Conference, Durban, South Africa, July 2000.

[40] For the most comprehensive analysis of how Mbeki used the occasion of his speech at Saartjie's funeral to make a position statement on HIV/AIDS, see Hoad, 'Thabo Mbeki's AIDS Blues'.

[41] For a full account and a legal and medical analysis of the MTCT case, its attendant issues and its broader political implications, see Mark Heywood, 'Preventing Mother-to-Child HIV Transmission in South Africa: Background, Strategies and Outcomes of the Treatment Action Campaign Case against the Minister of Health', *South African Journal of Human Rights*, 19 (2003), pp. 278–315. Further documentation relating to the case is also available at www.tac.org.za.

12 AFTERLIFE

[1] Cited in Iain Bamforth, ed., *The Body in the Library: A Literary Anthology of Modern Medicine* (London, 2003), p. ix.

[2] Sigmund Freud, 'The Question of Lay Analysis' (1926), in James Strachey and Anna Freud, eds, *The Standard Edition of the Complete Psychological Works*, vol. 20, (London, 1959).

[3] Felipe Fernandez-Armesto, *So You Think You're Human? A Brief History of Mankind* (Oxford, 2004), p. 84.

[4] Ibid., p. 89.

[5] Davies, *The Return of El Negro*, p. 52.

[6] Ibid.

[7] Thirty years later, the discovery of mitochondrial DNA (mtDNA) made it possible to work out the relatedness between different populations of people and to date the divergence of their ancestors. Studies analysing mtDNA have now concluded that modern humans began in Africa, probably just south of the Sahara. Somewhere in the region, that is, originally inhabited by the Khoisan.

[8] 'Sarah Baartman Funeral', 9 August 2002, South African Broadcasting Corporation, 63323–4.

[9] Mbeki, 'Speech at the Funeral of Sarah Baartman'. One of these

psychological legacies is a suspicion of Western science and medicine, whose racist legacy Mbeki attempted to use as validation for his government's refusal to fulfil its responsibility to provide medicines and treatment for those with HIV and AIDS.

[10] Morrison, *Playing in the Dark*, p. 24.

[11] Makhumandile 'Trompies' Bantom had been kidnapped and murdered for his 150,000 rand inheritance by Ayanda Kwinana, now serving a life sentence.

[12] The *Sarah Baartman* is the flagship of a series of four patrol vessels named after women who are synonymous with the struggle for freedom and the restoration of dignity for South African people. The other three ships are the *Lilian Ngoyi*, *Ruth First* and *Victoria Mxenge*. Saartjie's inclusion as a historical grandmother among these great twentieth-century leaders testifies to her cultural and political status in contemporary South Africa.

ACKNOWLEDGEMENTS

For assisting me in discovering the original research on which this biography is based, my thanks go to archivists Jackson Zweliyanyikima Vena, Cory Library, Rhodes University, Grahamstown; Erica Le Roux, Cape Town Archives Repository; and Mike Bevan, National Maritime Museum, Greenwich. I am grateful to Geoffrey Robinson, parish clerk and head verger, for his advice and instruction on the parish registers in Manchester Cathedral Archives, and for his generous welcome to the cathedral. Other important sources included the collections of the Museum Africa, Johannesburg; the National Library of South Africa, Cape Town; the Archives of the Royal Society London; the Royal College of Surgeons of England Library and Archive; the Wellcome Library for the History and Understanding of Medicine; the British Library; the London Library; the Colindale Newspaper Library; Lambeth Palace Library; the National Archives of the United Kingdom, Kew, Surrey; the Norfolk Record Office, Norwich; the Bibliothèque nationale de France; and the Muséum national d'histoire naturelle, Paris. Thanks and gratitude to friends and colleagues for additional research, translations and sharing their experience, insight, and expertise, particularly: Zackie Achmat, Jean Blanckenberg, Lucilla Blankenberg, Deena Bosch, Polly Clayden, Nadia Davids,

Heather Ewing, Nathan Geffen, Mark Gevisser, Nonkosi Khumalo, Jack Lewis, Bill and Jeanine Mitchell, Sipho Mthathi, Margie Oxford, Margaret Reynolds, Daffyd Roberts, Robert Symonds, and Shirley Thompson.

To the Ferreira sisters and the women at the Purple Orange Café in Hankey, my gratitude and respect for your warm and friendly welcome to a stranger. On legal questions I was patiently advised by Justice Edwin Cameron and Sadakat Kadri, to whom much appreciation.

Thank you Jackie Kay, Caroline Michel, Alexandra Pringle, and Bill Swainson.

For this new edition, my immense gratitude to Sarah Chalfant and Alba Ziegler-Bailey at The Wylie Agency and to Joel Arcanjo, Mike Fishwick, Lauren Whybrow and all the team at Bloomsbury.

INDEX

231

A NOTE ON THE TYPE

The text of this book is set in Bell. Originally cut for John Bell in 1788, this typeface was used in Bell's newspaper, The Oracle. It was regarded as the first English Modern typeface. This version was designed by Monotype in 1932.

'Sylvia Pankhurst was protesting that black lives matter before the term was invented. There would be no Greta Thunberg and no Malala Yousafzai were it not for Sylvia Pankhurst' Lemn Sissay

Sylvia Pankhurst's early years as one of the leaders of the suffragette movement developed into a lifetime's feminist work for equality and freedom. Seen as wild, even by the standards of her family, she lived a political life that spanned every key world event and movement from 1882 to 1960. And she wrote about it all, prolifically. She spent her life in dialogue, dispute, collision and resolution with Churchill, Lenin, Kenyatta, Selassie, Rama Rau and Keir Hardie, among others.

In this enthralling biography, Rachel Holmes interweaves Sylvia's rebellious public, private and secret lives to show how her astonishing career, long overlooked by historians, continues to resonate today.

'Sylvia Pankhurst was extraordinary. Rachel Holmes' biography of her is likewise extraordinary' Helen Pankhurst

'I have fallen in love with Sylvia Pankhurst. This is a masterpiece' Vanessa Redgrave

Order your copy:

By phone: +44 (0) 1256 302 699
By email: direct@macmillan.co.uk
Delivery is usually 3–5 working days.
Free postage and packaging for orders over £20.
Online: www.bloomsbury.com/bookshop
Prices and availability subject to change without notice.
https://www.bloomsbury.com/author/rachel-holmes/

THE SECRET LIFE OF DR JAMES BARRY

'A vivid and intelligent biography' *OBSERVER*

James Barry was one of the nineteenth century's most exceptional doctors, and one of its great unsung heroes. Famed for his brilliant innovations, Dr Barry influenced the birth of modern medical practice in places as far apart as South Africa, Jamaica and Canada. Barry's skills attracted admirers across the globe, but there were also many detractors of the ostentatious dandy, who caused controversy everywhere he went. Yet unbeknownst to all, the military surgeon concealed a lifelong secret at the heart of his identity: on his death Barry was claimed to be anatomically female and in fact a cross-dresser.

Vividly drawn and meticulously researched, *The Secret Life of Dr James Barry* brings to life one of the most enigmatic figures of the Victorian age, elevating its subject to a latter-day transgender icon – and is a landmark in the art of biography.

'Serious, sympathetic and absolutely fascinating'
MAIL ON SUNDAY

Order your copy:

By phone: +44 (0) 1256 302 699
By email: direct@macmillan.co.uk
Delivery is usually 3–5 working days.
Free postage and packaging for orders over £20.
Online: www.bloomsbury.com/bookshop
Prices and availability subject to change without notice.
https://www.bloomsbury.com/author/rachel-holmes/